NOT FAR *from the* **TREE**

VIGNETTES FROM LIVES WELL-LIVED

Paul E. White

Table of Contents

Dedication

To the Brackette family of Alabama, sharecroppers, my mother, Lillian Olivia (Brackette) White, who was the Brackette matriarch for many years, and to my father, William Clarence White, who was a self-made Renaissance man who took his life from poverty and despair to living the American Dream.

Acknowledgment

Everyone I have crossed paths with on my journey has, in some way, large or small, contributed to the stories shared in this book.

About the Author

Born to an African American father and Native American mother, the author grew up with an identity crisis in America of the 1940s and 1950s that was grappling with its racial past and the challenge of continuing on its path toward freedom and equality for all. In Not Far from the Tree, the author shares how his family broke free from the vicious cycle of poverty, dependency, and failure that entraps many in a web of hopelessness. He reveals an alternative to division and hate, a path based on unity and love.

ACORNS

"Acorns don't fall far from the tree." That adage says children often look like, exhibit behaviors, and have qualities, talents, or faults like their parents.

In this book, I will start with a popular internet post that briefly describes life growing up in my hometown of Brazil, Indiana, in the 1940s. I will then describe my parents and their lives in America in the early 1900s, my growing up in the 1940s and 1950s in Brazil, Indiana, and, in the book's final section, a few life adventures I had in Asia during the Cold War.

The series of vignettes was written at various times for different purposes. They do not necessarily follow one after the other in an orderly or systematic way. However, they are about the same person – me - so there are unifying crosscurrents and themes.

My plan is to complete two more books. The second will cover my 40-year career as a Foreign Service Officer, and the third will cover my life after retirement from the U.S. State Department. A unifying theme will be my parents' incredible accomplishments, resilience, and teaching, and the fact that acorns fall close to the oak tree that produced them.

My life is a tribute to that of my parents, who sacrificed so much to advance my chances of having a life better than theirs.

LIFE IN BRAZIL, INDIANA – The 1940s

There is a post that is often seen on the World Wide Web. A version of it was posted on FaceBook by a childhood friend from Brazil, Indiana, Warren Woodall, on June 17, 2022. It captures his and my 1940s childhood experiences growing up in a rural Indiana town.

I grew up in Brazil, Indiana, where almost everyone treated each other with respect.

We didn't eat much fast food because it was considered a treat, not a food group. We drank Kool-Aid from water from our kitchen sink with real sugar. We ate bologna sandwiches, or even tuna (which was in a can not a pouch), grilled cheese sandwiches, and hot dogs. We mostly ate home-cooked meals consisting of meat, potatoes, vegetables, bread, butter, and homemade desserts.

We grew up during a time when we mowed lawns, pulled weeds, babysat, and helped neighbors with chores to earn our own money. We went outside a lot to play kickball, fish, swim, ride bikes, throw frisbees, and run with friends. We played baseball, basketball, football, hide and seek, jump rope, jacks, and marbles.

We drank tap water from the water hose outside... bottled water was unheard of. If we had a Pepsi or Coke - it was in a glass bottle... and we didn't break the bottle when finished, we took it to the store to get pennies in exchange. That was recycling before its time.

We watched TV shows like The Jefferson's, Good Times, Mork & Mindy, M*A*S*H, Gilligan's Island, Happy Days, Bewitched, Looney Tunes cartoons, the Flintstones, the Jetsons, Dukes of Hazzard, I Dream of Jeannie, the Twilight Zone, and I Love Lucy.

After school, we would rush home to watch the Mickey Mouse Club and Dick Clark's American Bandstand on tiny screen black and white TVs. Then we did homework and chores. When finished, we would go outside with friends to play under the streetlights or under the stars.

We would ride our bikes for hours. The three rules were that we had to tell our parents where we were going, whom we were going with, and we had to come home when it was dark! Otherwise, we were on our own to boldly explore far and wide.

We LEARNED from our parents instead of disrespecting them and treating them as if they knew absolutely nothing. What they said was LAW. We did not question it. And once told something, we had better remember it, understand it, and respect it!!!

In school, we said the Pledge of Allegiance. We stood for the National Anthem. We said prayers in church, and there were Sunday School lessons. We listened to our teachers. I also remember that we would go to school movies on some Friday evenings. On some Saturdays, after our chores were done, we would walk to Main Street to a movie theater with our friends to watch cowboy movies like Roy Rogers, Gene Autry, or The Lone Ranger. There were always lots of Tom and Jerry, Bugs Bunny, Woody Woodpecker, and other cartoons to make us laugh.

On Sunday, we had to go to Sunday School and Church Service, and then back home, we would have Sunday dinner with the entire family around the same table.

We were told to be seen, not heard, if we got too loud. We watched what we said around our elders because we knew if we DISRESPECTED any grown-up, we would get our behinds spanked or our mouths washed out with soap. That wasn't called abuse back in the day; it was called discipline!

We held doors open for girls, women, and those older than us. We carried groceries to help others. We gave up our seats on public transport for women and older people without being asked.

You wouldn't hear curse words on the radio, in songs, or on TV because cursing was not allowed on the airways and certainly not in our homes. If we cursed and got caught, that was a clarion call for soap in your mouth to wash away the nastiness.

Words like "Please. Thank you. Yes, please. No, thank you. Yes ma'am. No ma'am. Yes sir. No sir" were all part of our daily lexicon and vocabulary! Those words of respect were said to everyone who deserved respect – anyone a little older than we were. We grew up

5

respecting our Nation and Old Glory - the flag of the United States of America. We would stand with respect when the flag was brought into a room. In school, we would put our hands over our hearts to say the Pledge. We would close our eyes and bow our heads to say prayers.

We can be thankful for our childhood – growing up in the 1940s. I will never forget where I came from and wish children nowadays had half the chance to have the fun and respect for real life we had when we were growing up!

I love♥ how we lived back in the day in Brazil, Indiana. Those were the Days, my friend!

That describes the environment I grew up in. Next are true stories about the struggles and triumphs of two magnificent oak trees – my father, William Clarence White, and my mother, Lillian Olivia (Brackette) White. Life in the early 1900s was not easy for them.

Today, loud voices criticizing America's past and present drown out those with a different view. America's strength is its diversity is a false premise often used to incite division and hatred. This book shows that a family's self-reliance, confidence, resilience, and love rather than diversity, victimhood, despair, and hate results in success against the most difficult odds.

Three generations of stories about our family reveal how far America has come. While still imperfect, our family's history shows America's steady movement toward a more perfect union. America's National Motto – E Pluribus Unum (Out of Many One) shows that Unity (One), not Diversity (Many), has been and is America's strength.

The benefitted may be quiet, but their inspiring lives matter, as do their voices. They are not "exceptions to the rule"; they "are the rule!" In Acorns Fall Close to the Tree, I give voice to my family's remarkable journey. Younger family members can know and appreciate the journey and learn that while diversity is noble, it leads to destruction when paired with division and hate. In the context of unity and love, success is achieved.

Acorns falling close to the tree mean strong families produce strong children who make America and the world better places.

COAL MINES TO HOT SPRINGS

In 1890, my father, William Clarence White, was born "dirt-poor" in Harriman, Roane County, Tennessee. His father, my grandfather, Daniel White, was born a slave. After the Civil War and Lincoln's Emancipation Proclamation, Daniel took a job that paid little but stressed his body a lot. He worked mining coal and ore in the Appalachian coal fields of eastern Tennessee.

Daniel's son wanted to learn to read and write as a child, but in rural Tennessee at the time, there were few schools for people of color. In 1900, a member of a black church began a program to teach "colored children" to read and write. But at ten years of age, my father was already working in the coal mines. He could not attend that church school. He grew up illiterate, just as his father, Daniel, had been before him.

In the mine, my father worked as a "mule." Kids often tended the mules of burden used to pull coal cars on tracks up from the dark depth of the mine. Small children could also access and mine coal veins too tight for a grown man to enter.

There were no child labor laws, so many young kids, black and white, worked in the mines. Life was difficult for them. They toiled in the dark, dusty depths of the earth for 15 hours at a time.

It was "all work, no play" in that shadowy world. Their only future was to work in the mine until they were too old, tired, sick, or weak to keep working.

Around 1902, on a tragic day, there was an explosion in the depth of the mine. Many miners were killed. My grandfather, Daniel White, was not in the mine on that sad day, but his son - my father - Clarence, was working there. Daniel rushed to the devastation. He watched helplessly as the injured and dead miners were carried from the mine. Finally, he saw his young son, Clarence, being carried from the mine on a makeshift stretcher. Clarence was alive but had suffered a debilitating injury – a broken back.

When I was young, my father recalled what his father said to him as he was carried on the stretcher. Daniel leaned toward him and said, *"Son, that is perhaps the best thing that could ever have happened to you."*

I asked, *"Why would Grandpa Daniel say that to his son?"*

My father explained, *"He meant that I would never be able to work manual labor again. I would have to find a way to make a living with something other than my brute strength. That would be a blessing."* He emphasized, *"My father meant that my days of hard labor in the dark depth of a mine were over and done with!"*

Grandpa Daniel White was right. After a long and painful recovery, my father never returned to that coal mine. He regained the ability to walk but walked with a bent back and limp for the rest of his life. Still, he considered himself fortunate. He was alive, and he eventually found a job that did not require his brawn.

In 1905, he began working in a local piano store. In America in the early 1900s, there were no movie theaters, television sets, or internet entertainment like we have today. Entertainment was hard to come by, especially in rural areas. Pianos were one popular form of entertainment. They could be found in almost every church, school, and home, and piano stores were found even in the smallest towns.

My father's main job at the piano store was janitorial. He was paid to sweep the floors, dust, carry firewood and water to the store, and perform other menial tasks. He was given one piano-related task - piano stringer.

When the pianos arrived at the store from a distant piano factory, my father's job was to put the strings on each piano. He would put the short, small-gauged treble strings on the pins at the top of the sounding board and the long, heavy-gauged strings on the pins at the bass side of the sounding board.

Stringing a piano did not take any special training or skill, and it was not very time-consuming. But it was an essential prelude to a more prestigious job – piano tuning.

The store employed a German piano tuner. After my father finished stringing the pianos, the tuner adjusted each string of the eighty-eight keys using a tuning wrench until they were all in perfect tune.

While doing his other chores at the store, my father would watch the tuner tighten and tune the strings. He would listen to the tuner combine notes and adjust the strings until the piano was in perfect tune.

One day, in perhaps 1907, an opportunity came along that my father could not resist pursuing. Several new pianos arrived at the store. My father strung the pianos as he always did. The German tuner was out sick. My father waited until the store owner was away from the store to go boldly where he had never been before. "Borrowing" the German's tuning tools, my father proceeded to tune the newly arrived pianos. Even though he had no training, my father was confident about his work. He did everything just the way he had observed over many months.

When the piano tuner recovered from the flu and returned to the store, he was surprised to find that the new pianos were in good tune. Concerned about his job, the tuner asked the store owner, *"Did these here pianos arrive from the factory already tuned?"*

"No," the store owner answered, adding. *"They arrived unstrung, but Clarence did an excellent job stringing 'em up, just like he always does."*

The tuner was relieved but curious. He cast a side glance at my father, who gave him a sheepish look. The tuner instantly knew what had happened. He was furious but did not say anything until the store owner left.

Alone with my father, the tuner's face turned as red as a beet. Towering over my father, the tuner shouted, *"Hey, boy! Did you pilfer with my tools? You had no right to touch them! What a mess you have left these here pianos in! Get the hell out of here!"*

Later that day, the tuner called my father back into the store. To protect his job, he had come up with a plan. *"Boy, you've got a God-*

11

given talent for tuning. I don't know how you did it, but these pianos here are tuned to snuff – better than I could do. But there ain't no room in this here store nor town for two tuners. I'm gonna give you a tuning fork, a tuning wrench, and some other tools. Take them and get out of town – tonight. Or..., I can get you into a boatload of trouble."

My father accepted the gifted tools, left, and never returned to that piano store. An enterprising young man, my father soon used his talent and new tools to tune pianos in black churches in several small towns. He would ask the church musicians to teach him to play the piano in exchange for his tuning service and always ask if he could stay for a few hours to practice playing.

He had a natural gift for music, was a fast learner, and soon outpaced his teachers. By 1909, word of my father's talent had spread rapidly. He was in high demand as a church pianist. That took him to larger towns and eventually from rural Tennessee to Louisville, Kentucky.

In Louisville, he played not just in black churches but also in black dives and black eating places. By 1912, silent movies were having a heyday. But they were not so silent. A talented piano player could make good money playing an accompaniment to the silent movie's action. The piano player could use music to make the audience hear and feel the joy, sadness, excitement, and other emotions being acted on screen by the silent movie actors and actresses.

My father was so good at capturing the emotions portrayed on the silent screen that by 1915, he was fully occupied as a musician. He played in movie theaters, black churches, black bars, and for black parties and social gatherings.

In 1917, he was hired by an exclusive white resort, the Greenbriar Resort in West Virginia. That changed his life forever because that was where he met my mother, Lillian Olivia Brackette.

Lillian was of Creek Indian heritage, born in 1897 near the Tombigbee River in southwestern Alabama. At 20, she left

Alabama, seeking a better life. She found work as a maid at the Greenbriar Resort, where she met the piano player Clarence White.

My mother once told me, *"I never saw a man as tall and handsome as your father, and then I heard him play the piano. Could that man play? He was a music genius!"*

Infatuated with the tall, dark, and handsome piano-playing black man with the unusual name White, they began to date. In 1918, they married and started planning a new chapter—a new life far from the bigoted and opportunity-denying South.

My father had long been a gypsy. From the time he left his home in Tennessee with just a piano tuning wrench and tuning fork, he had moved from town to town, playing the piano as his significant profession and tuning pianos when there was an opportunity.

But Clarence had never met a restless gypsy like my mother. She had left her home hoping to better herself. When she met Clarence, she saw a way forward to realize her dream of moving from the South. Together, they began to plan their new life.

Lillian said, and what she said was true, *"I was, I am, and I shall always be a wayward wind that longs to wander."*

WAYWARD WINDS IN A MODEL T FORD

Neither Clarence nor Lillian had much money, but by pooling their savings, they were able to purchase a used Model T Ford. It was sold as junk because it had been in an accident. Clarence spent weeks seeking parts and repairing the Model T. As he worked on the car, my mother planned their "getaway" from the life-limiting and bigoted South.

Lillian had told Clarence about her Uncle Eddie. Uncle was a term of affinity for Native Americans. Eddie was perhaps not a blood relative, but was of the same Creek Indian clan as my mother. An older man of the same clan was always called "uncle."

From her girlhood, my mother had heard stories about Uncle Eddie. He was a folk legend. Eddie had worked as a cook for a placer gold mine in Alabama. With the discovery of gold in California in 1849, many Alabama gold miners left Alabama's gold fields to seek their fortune in California.

Uncle Eddie left Alabama with a group of Gold Rushers. As his story was told, he bragged to his Creek Indian clan and friends that he would return to Alabama with gold in his teeth and pockets.

Uncle Eddie was never heard of again. My mother's dream was to go to California because once there, she might learn "the rest of Uncle Eddie's story."

My father and mother began a quest to head west, seeking a golden place that offered much-desired individual freedom and the opportunity to grow and prosper. They planned to go from town to town. In a new town, my father would tune and play the piano while my mother worked as a maid. They would save money in each town until they had enough to move to the next town.

The times were good. Over a year or more, they made it from West Virginia to Kentucky, always moving westward, one town at a time. When they reached a new town, my mother would find work as a maid. My father would attend church, play the piano, and quickly find places to play and pianos to tune.

When business slowed, or they had enough money for gas and food, they continued their gypsy ways, always heading westward.

My father became a specialist at working black churches, dives, and restaurants. But a much larger market was the white public schools and white churches that he did not have access to because he was black. Getting accepted in the white market was against social norms and mores, not only in the South but more generally in America at that day and time.

Occasionally, my father would tune a piano for a white client. It was usually through personal contact—often a black minister in a church where my father had tuned contacted a white minister friend who needed a piano tuned. Those rare occasions whetted my father's appetite to find a way to regularly gain access to the much larger white piano tuning market. Because he was so talented, my father began making small inroads into white churches, white public schools, and some white businesses.

Word of mouth was his best advertisement in the highly segregated and race-conscious America of the 1920s and 1930s. Although difficult, he slowly gained access to some white churches and schools, which gave him limited access to another large and untapped market—pianos in white-family homes.

Except in a rare happenstance, the white home market was almost impossible to access for a black piano tuner. During weekdays, the man of the house would be in the fields if he was a farmer or otherwise at work away from home. That would leave the housewife at home alone or with her children. Being alone with a white woman was "verboten" for a black man.

But my always creative father conceived of an ingenious socially- and psychologically sound solution. He hired a white man named Rowe. Rowe's job was to be my father's "front man." Rowe would knock on a door. *"Excuse me, ma'am, do you have a piano?"*

"Yes."

"Does it need a good tuning?"

"Yes, it is way out of tune! And it is in awful shape."

16

"Well, I am here to help you get it repaired and tuned - at a reasonable price by one of the best tuners in the business today!"

The housewife and Rowe would agree on a price. Rowe then used his most convincing voice to say, "But there's just one thing. I'm not a piano tuner. You see that black fellow out there in the Model T? He is the piano tuner. And he is a darn good one!"

Rowe would quickly add, "But you don't have to worry nary a single strand of hair on your head; I have a pistol right here in this holster. Nothing will go wrong. We are here (he would point at his pistol) to guarantee that."

As silly as that ploy sounds today, back in that day, it worked wonders. Rowe had a very innocent face, voice, and demeanor. In many cases, but not all, private home doors would swing open. It was then on my father's shoulders to succeed by seizing on and making the opportunity work to expand his piano tuning business.

Years later, my father reminisced about those heady times with frontman Rowe. Father told me, "Paul, don't ever give up. Where there's a will, there's a way! You just have to be the best and prove it!"

My father did more than gain access. He developed a marketing strategy that assured organic growth for his business. Before he began to tune, he would give a well-practiced and very respectful pitch to the housewife, "Excuse me, ma'am, please do invite your family and friends to come over. They can watch me tune your piano. They will enjoy it. And they will be in for a real treat at the end."

As he had intimated, the best part came after the tuning was over.

When he finished tuning, my father would announce to the gathered audience, "Now, for the fun part – a concert with a purpose. I'm going to play five musical numbers that test every note on the piano multiple times in every possible combination of notes. When I finish, I will know that all 88 keys work as they should and that the piano is tuned to Carnegie Hall standards."

That was perhaps hyperbole, but it allowed my father to showcase his remarkable piano-playing genius. He believed the audience listening to him would tout his tuning and piano-playing skills to their family and friends. They did just that.

My father had a stirring 5-song repertoire for the mini-concert. First, he would play a popular song of that time. Then, a syncopated ragtime song. Ragtime was extremely popular in the early 1900s. Next was a John Phillip Sousa march. Then, another popular song. He would always end with a religious song.

The ragtime song got everyone's feet tapping. Then, he began to play a military march medley. It started with Stars and Stripes Forever. In the middle of the rousing Stars and Stripes march, my father would play on the highest treble notes, making the piano sound like a piccolo. Then, his two hands would descend to the lowest bass notes, rolling over them in a percussive way that made them sound just like a marching band's drum corps.

If that were not enough, in that march medley, my father would include the military songs - the Caissons Song for the Army, then Anchors Away for the Navy, The Wild Blue Yonder for the Air Force, and the Marine Hymn for the Marines. People were patriotic back in the day, and they simply loved that medley.

The best was saved for last. Using his church music-playing skills, which started him in the music business, my father's fifth song of his repertoire was *"The Old Rugged Cross."* My father had mastered a "trill" technique that gave the well-known hymn both melodic and rhythmic richness.

The trilling made the piano sound like a mandolin. That, combined with my father's caressing touch on the keys, made the music reach out and touch the hearts of believers and non-believers alike. Some were moved to tears. That song alone would ensure that my father would be invited to play the piano at a local church service, further expanding his contacts and future piano tuning business opportunities in white churches.

After being thoroughly entertained, the word about my father's piano skills would spread like wildfire. My father's "front man" strategy, combined with his mini-concert marketing technique, gave the tuner and his pistol-totting front man lots of business. Doors were opened that would never have been earlier.

My father's reputation as an excellent tuner, dependable businessman, and safe person to have in a home or business went surging ahead of him - from house to house, community to community, and town to town. Music teachers and piano stores were really good at getting the word out, as were churches.

As good as things were, trouble was brewing for my father and mother. Around 1926, they arrived in a new town in a new state— Vincennes, Indiana. Vincennes was proving more lucrative than any place they had been. My mother found a job as a maid and babysitter for a wealthy family. The Schultize family loved her, and she loved them.

My father met a contact during his first few days in Vincennes. The contact connected him to black and white churches and the public school system.

The business was so good that they decided it was time to start a family. They did not give up on California but temporarily put the Golden State destination on hold. In 1928, after a couple of years in Vincennes, my father had saved enough money to buy new clothes and put a cash down payment on a house. They retired Front Man Rowe as he was no longer needed.

Life in Vincennes was good for the Whites - until it was not!

Thrilled that they were growing and prospering, that big decision had not come easy, but they were tired of the grind of being "on the road." The down payment was a commitment to Vincennes, and the two gypsies looked forward to starting a family in this city on the banks of the fabled Wabash River.

How proud Clarence and Lillian were to own their own home! But a few months after moving in, they heard angry shouts coming from their front yard just as they were going to bed.

My father cautiously opened the front door. He was confronted by a drunken mob of 30 or 40 men cloaked in white robes shouting obscenities. Some wore and were flashing firearms.

"Nigger, who do you think you are.? What are you doing in our town? We don't want you and your woman here in Vincennes! Get the hell out of Vincennes tonight, or you'll be sorry."

Pointing to the burning cross on the lawn, the drunk men threatened, *"Nigger, we'll burn your house down with you and your woman in it! Get out now if you want to live to see another day!"*

Indiana was the largest Ku Klux Klan state outside of the Solid South. Half of the state legislature proudly said they were KKK. It was the home to a Grand Dragon of the KKK. My father did not know what he had done, but later learned the rest of the story.

His growing piano tuning business in Vincennes was causing grief to an elderly white piano tuner. The not-very-skilled tuner was blind. He was losing much of his business to the "new tuner in town." After learning that his competitor was black, the blind tuner appealed to his KKK friends for help.

Burning a cross on the lawn, ugly name-calling, and threatening death was a game-changer. My father and mother threw a few belongings in the Model T and left their house and most of what they owned, escaping into the dark night.

Terrorized, they left a note on the front porch of the Shultize family's house, where Lillian worked as a maid, explaining why they left Vincennes. They drove northward into the night, not knowing where they were going or what would happen next.

They did not doubt that the threats were real and that their lives would have been taken had they stayed. Fearful of what had just transpired in Vincennes, my father wanted to put Indiana in the rearview mirror as soon as possible. He knew first-hand what an angry white mob could do.

As a child, he saw a group of white boys use baseball bats to club his younger brother, Romie, for looking at a white girl the "wrong way." Romie fell into a coma and died.

In that brutal beating and murder, the police were never called because that would have only put the family under more suspicion and would not have brought Romie back.

An hour or two after leaving Vincennes, Clarence and Lillian arrived at Terre Haute, Indiana, also on the Wabash River. For some reason, rather than following the road west, they turned east, driving for some 15 miles to a small town named Brazil. They slept in Brazil that night in the Model T.

My mother felt Vincennes would have been a good place to raise a family. Despite the problem with the KKK, she still believed that Indiana would be a good place to settle. She probably suggested to her husband that they should at least give Brazil a chance.

Lillian must have won the discussion. The next day, instead of heading westward, they stayed in Brazil and immediately began their usual routine of looking for employment.

In the 1930s, Brazil was a small but bustling town. Located between Indianapolis and Terre Haute on the National Road (Highway 40), Brazil was a natural stopping place for travelers going west or east. Along Brazil's Main Street, there were hotels, restaurants, banks, a 5 & 10-cent store, grocery stores, furniture stores, and even a piano store.

Brazil's soil was fertile for farming and rich in minerals. Brazil named itself the "Clay Center of the World." There were vast deposits of high-quality clay. Brazil was well known for having eight kinds of clay sought after for architectural tile and impervious-facing brick. In the 1930s, Brazil and its surrounding communities had 11 clay mines and factories that provided good employment to thousands.

Brazil also had easy access to coal. It had 13 companies mining bituminous coal, which was located closer to the surface than anthracite coal. Bituminous coal can be mined with cheaper "strip

21

pit" operations rather than the more costly deep-earth mines needed to mine anthracite coal.

Bituminous coal is mainly burned to generate electricity, produce heat for industrial processes, and make coke for steel production. Because of that use, Brazil had 13 coal mines and three steel plants near them.

High industrial employment in the clay mines, architectural tile factories, coal mines, and steel plants made Brazil a boom town. The town supported such luxuries as hand-rolled cigar and piano factories.

My mother quickly found employment. She began working as a maid for several wealthy families. Brazil was a piano tuner's paradise. Clarence's business immediately soared, and this time, my father checked to see that there were no blind competitors that he might put out of business.

My father's excellent reputation, congenial personality, and piano-playing talent were in high demand. People in Brazil were friendly and grateful to have a piano tuner in their midst.

Schools immediately hired Clarence, and churches were responsive to him. The home market was open to him, and his business grew.

My father and mother decided to take a chance again. They put money down on a house in this bustling little town. They did not forsake their original plan of going to California but the plan was put on hold again so they could start and raise a family.

In 1930, Clarence and Lillian purchased a house at 754 North Columbia Street in what was called "Stringtown." The lives of two wayward wind gypsies became less willful and more predictable. The Whites again tried to settle down and start a family. They were happy to call the busy little town in southwest Indiana with the funny name - Brazil – their new "Home Sweet Home."

W.C. White doing what he loved - tuning

Home Sweet Home early 1930s – 754 North Columbia Street, Brazil Indiana

Two magnificent oak trees

CHILDHOOD AND COLD WAR
VIGNETTES

Those are a few of many stories about my remarkable oak tree parents. In the following section, I will present personal vignettes from my life.

First, I will cover my birth and three vignettes from early non-school learning. Those vignettes will be followed by five vignettes about my Cold War non-military service as a volunteer and as a Department of State civilian Foreign Service Officer in Laos and Cambodia during the Vietnam War.

Brazil's school system was phenomenal. I attended Alabama Street Grade School, Meridian Street Middle School, and Brazil Junior High and Senior High School. I played trombone in the band, was a co-captain of an undefeated Brazil Red Devils football team, was captain of an undefeated track team, and was an Honor Society student. Except for a few name-calling bigots, my classmates and teachers were friendly, supportive, and terrific. After graduating high school in 1959, I attended several colleges.

In 1964, I graduated from Valparaiso University in Indiana with a dual major in psychology and philosophy. At graduation, I received a full congressional fellowship to the University of Hawaii's East-West Center Asian Studies graduate program.

In 1979, I was awarded a mid-career graduate fellowship at Stanford University. My major was Social Change in the Third World.

My life was blessed. I received the education both my mother and father deserved but never had. My parents sacrificed much to help me secure a good education, which led to a dream career.

In 1966, I went to Laos as a volunteer with International Voluntary Services (IVS). IVS was a thriving international volunteer program. It was the model used by President Kennedy to design the U.S. Peace Corps.

After IVS, I continued to work in Laos with the U.S. Department of State's Agency for International Development (USAID). I started my USAID career as a Refugee Relief and Rehabilitation Officer. During my 40-year foreign service career, I worked on four continents and learned a dozen languages.

After vignettes about my birth in Brazil and some early learning from my 1940s childhood, five vignettes will follow, covering my experiences in Laos and Cambodia in the 1970s during the Vietnam War.

TOO STUBBORN TO LEAVE

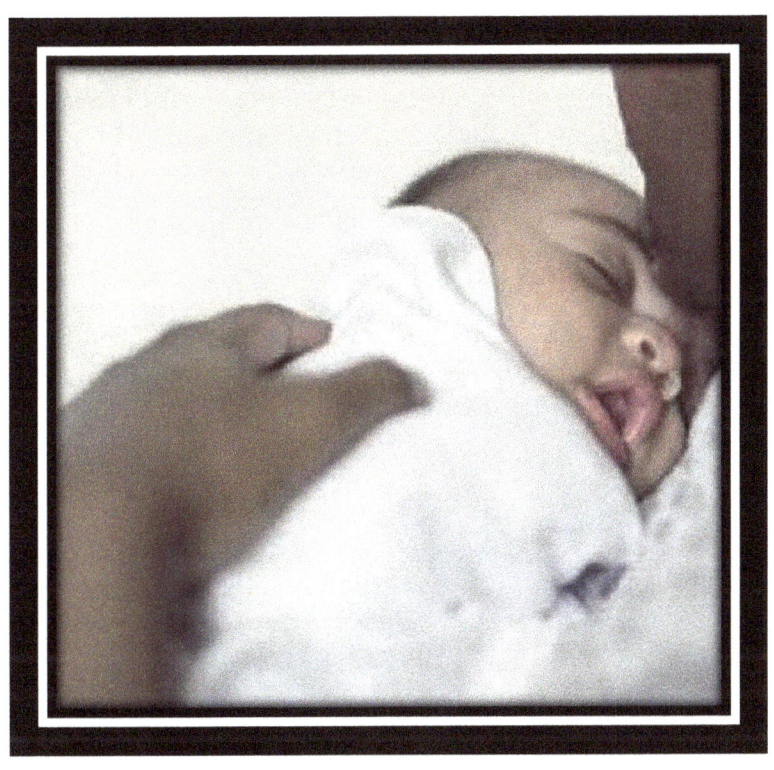

It is told that on a cold, cloudless, moonless March night in 1768, Shawnee Indian Chief Puckshinwah looked at the multitude of stars arrayed against a vast purple-black canopy of Ohio night sky. The stars were so bright they seemed alive.

Puckshinwah's campfire had died, leaving a few smoldering red-orange embers in a scatter of grey-white ash. Puckshinwah felt the cold quietness of that night in the depth of his being. A muffled cry broke the silence. Puckshinwah's wife – Turtle Laying Eggs in the Sand – had just given birth.

As he heard the baby's cry, Puckshinwah's eyes were drawn to the heavens, where the brilliant light of a massive comet burned a green-white path from North to South across the sky. Its bright light cast Puckshinwah's shadow on the scattered ashes of the spent campfire. For the Shawnee tribe, shooting stars were an auspicious omen – thought to be a Great Spirit called The Panther.

Puckshinwah paced in the cold, wanting to see his newborn. Finally, the squaw attending his wife called, *"Chief, it's a boy-child. You have a son."*

In Shawnee culture, newborn babies were not named for at least ten days, but the synchronism of this birth with the comet's sudden appearance dictated an immediate naming. After all, a Great Spirit had witnessed the birth of Shawnee Chief Puckshinwah's son.

Puckshinwah named his son after the burning comet – "Panther Passing Across." In the Shawnee language, Panther Passing Across is translated as a single word - *"Tecumseh."*

Fast forward to 1941 – also in the Midwest – this time one state away from Ohio - Indiana. Piano tuner William Clarence White was nicknamed Whitey because of his premature shock of white hair. Whitey's wife was in labor. Whitey was waiting for the birth of their child in an adjacent room of their house.

Whitey's wife was a Native American of the Muskogee Creek tribe. Her nickname was Bay. Bay had carried to full term and delivered eight children before this one. All eight were boys. All eight were stillborn or had died within a few days of birth.

Whitey and Bay were now middle-aged. This would be their last attempt to have a child. Whitey hand-rolled and chain-smoked one cigarette after another. As he drew deeply on his hand-rolled Prince Albert tobacco cigarette, the tobacco burned with a red-orange glow. He exhaled soft grey-white smoke. The smoke hung in the humid, stifling, hot August air. Smoking was a brief but satisfying respite for Whitey, an escape from his all-consuming anxiety.

A muffled cry broke the silence. The baby had arrived. Whitey wanted to rush into the room, but he knew he should wait for the midwife. Whitey rolled and smoked another cigarette. Then another. Finally, a midwife called, *"It's a boy. You can come in now."*

Entering the room, Whitey saw his wife, Bay, holding a beautiful baby boy. The baby's loud crying let the world know he was alive. But Whitey and Bay were tense. They restrained their joy. There had been eight disappointments. Too many deaths. They fervently prayed for this baby boy to stay with them.

Tension also showed on the faces of those in the room – not just Bay and Whitey, but also two neighborhood midwives.

A loud knock at the front door interrupted the nervous tension. A midwife rushed to the front door. *"Why, Dr. Sourwine, please come in. The baby is already here."*

Like the eight previous babies, this one was also born at home because the Clay County Hospital in Brazil, Indiana, in the 1940s, was "for whites only. Doctor Sourwine stopped by to attend this birth because Bay worked for the Sourwine family as a housemaid. The doctor could not attend her at the hospital, but he had agreed to stop by and help with the birth at Bay's home – 754 North Columbia Street.

Doctor Sourwine took his time examining the newborn. Everyone held their breath. With each passing minute, the tension built. Finally, Doctor Sourwine turned, cleared his throat, looked at Bay and Whitey, and said, *"Lillian,"* – he used Bay's given name – *"your baby boy is ..... as healthy as a horse."*

Laughter filled the room at the good news and the country doctor's use of colloquial language. Bay and Whitey had stopped naming their babies after the first few deaths. Having a name made each loss even more painful.

But this time, Bay courageously told her husband, *"This baby boy is magic! A name for this magic boy should follow the doctor's good news."*

Bay confidently said, *"Let's name this magic boy Paul - after Paul Robeson."* Paul Robeson was a highly educated black baritone singer, professional football player, movie star, labor activist, and flaming Communist. *"How ironic, my namesake was a Communist!"*

Yes, that magic birth child - Paul – was and is me – Paul Edward White. Now you know why magic has been with me since my first breath. Named Paul after a communist and Edward after my mother's Uncle Eddie. Eddie was a Creek Indian who left the Alabama homeland in 1849, heading to California to find gold. Uncle Eddie was never heard of again,

With the given names -Paul and Edward, I had two name-related skeletons in my closet. Could there be more?

You are probably wondering why this vignette began with a story about the birth of Tecumseh. There is a direct connection that yields a third name-related skeleton. It is a long but true story.

In the 1760s, Chief Puckshinwah's Great Lakes Shawnee Indian tribe was in exile in Alabama, driven from their Ohio Valley homeland by the Iroquois – a warring rival tribe. While in exile in Alabama, Puckshinwah married a Creek Indian maiden named Methotaske (Turtle Laying Eggs in the Sand).

That is the connection. Like my mother, Bay, Methotaske was a Muskogee Creek Indian. They were of a different time, for sure, but both were born into the same tribe and clan—the rebel Red Stick Creek Turtle clan of the Muskogee Creek nation.

It takes more story to reveal the skeleton. My mother always told me that Tecumseh was a great Creek chieftain, but he is described in all the history books as a Shawnee Chief. For years, I doubted my mother and was disappointed that she seemed not to know Tecumseh's tribal affiliation.

I finally resolved that large discrepancy. Native Americans track lineage matrilineally. Tecumseh's father was Shawnee, but his mother was Creek. For Native Americans, Tecumseh was a Creek. For American historians, who track lineage through the father, Tecumseh was a Shawnee. My mother was true to her culture. That is the third skeleton of my "checkered" past. By clan lineage, the fiercely anti-American freedom fighter Tecumseh is family – at least a clan relative! What an honor - having Chief Tecumseh in my distant family lineage!

That unlocks all my name-related skeletons. I was named after a Communist activist (Paul Robeson) and a gold-seeking opportunist (Eddie Brackette) who disappeared from the face of the earth. A third skeleton is a bloodline that is linked to Panther Passing Across— Tecumseh.

Tecumseh valiantly fought against American hero Old Hickory – General Andrew Jackson. Communist, disappeared 49er, and anti-American rebel - who could ask for any more skeletons in their closet?

For many years, I owned a Red Stick Creek warclub and a small single-shot hand-crafted rifle given to me by my mother. The war club was a lethal weapon when used against other Indian tribes in hand-to-hand combat, but "red sticks" were not very effective against American army rifles (thunder sticks). Eventually, rifles replaced war clubs and bows and arrows as the Indians' war weapons of choice.

The Red Stick warclub and rifle I own are valuable connections with my heritage. I treasure them even more after learning about the Red Stick Creek history and learning that the great Shawnee Chief Tecumseh was, as my mother had told me so many years ago, a Creek Indian Chief by Native American lineage.

My father used to say to me, *"Paul, I am glad you were too stubborn (he used the term onery) to leave us. If your eight brothers had been as onery as you were, I would have had a baseball team of sons."*

To make him smile, I would retort with, *"If I had been born with a voice like Paul Robeson, I might now be a flaming communist activist or a red stick rabble-rouser rather than a right-leaning American Foreign Service Officer!"*

Mother and me by the backyard lily pool

Bay and her younger sister, Emmie, with Emmie's six kids
(Marilyn and Hyla added)

Four Angels in Heaven – Watt (Dick), Lillian (Bay), Emmie,
and Annie

Dick, Bay, Emmie, Annie, and Dick's family in Alabama, circa 1955

Uncle Dick at 754 N. Columbia Street, circa 1950

Annie and Bay at 754 N. Columbia Street circa 1950

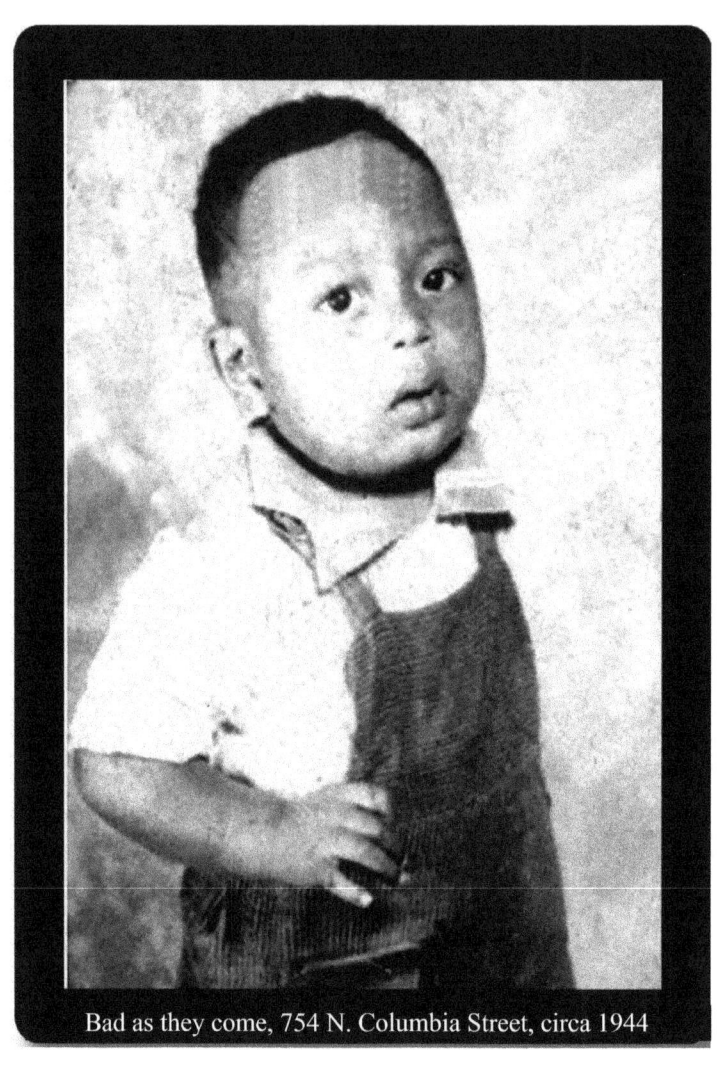

Bad as they come, 754 N. Columbia Street, circa 1944

Paul, Lillian, and Clarence, Idlewild, MI, circa 1957

Paul – Trombone playing fool – Jazz Band, circa 1958

Undefeated Brazil High Red Devils, Wasbish Valley Champs – 1958

TECUMSEH

In the first grade at Alabama Street School, the class was asked to talk about their ancestors. Kids talked about their German, Irish, Italian, French, or British heritage. I had no idea what to say. Fortunately, because my last name starts with W, I was sitting in the last row and was not called that day. At home that night, I asked my mother, *"What should I say?"* We had never talked about race or heritage.

"Tell that class that your father's ancestors came from Africa and that on your mother's side, they are American Indian. Don't be ashamed of that. Be proud." I did share my mother's message, but I am sure that the teacher and my classmates saw shame on my face and heard the hesitancy in my voice.

After that embarrassing incident, my mother began sharing with me stories about her family, upbringing, and heritage. Mainly, she taught me lessons she had learned from her grandmother. At an early age, my mother's mother, (Laura Brackette), died while giving birth. After Laura's death, my mother, her older brother, and two younger sisters were raised by Emma Brackette, their Muskogee Creek grandmother.

Mother taught me in what she called "Nature School." Mother had a kaleidoscopic knowledge of plants and animals. She tried to spend every day outside in Nature, and her teaching was based on the Native American belief that all plants and animals have meaning and spirit. Indians believe that with attention, humans can understand, learn from, and even communicate with plants, animals, and other elements of Nature like rocks, mountains, wind, and rain.

At the time, those lessons were difficult to understand. They were not expressed using words as I am now. They were taught to me while my mother was fishing on the banks of Deer Creek, hunting nuts and mushrooms, picking wild greens in Brown's woods, or gathering wild raspberries or blackberries in a farmer's back-nine.

My mother had a particular affinity for turtles. She would tell me, *"The lowly turtle is an important totem. I would love to be an eagle or wolf, but I am a turtle."* She would say, *"Little Paul, your mother was born to be and shall always be a turtle.*" That meant absolutely nothing to me. Those lessons now mean much more to me than they ever did when I was young.

My mother's word lessons were more direct. I understood them. Mother once said to me as she was burning leaves on a crisp autumn night, *"Little Paul, watch the smoke drift into the night sky toward the Great White River called the Milky Way. Our ancestors live in the sky along that Great White River. The drifting smoke forms a sacred trail. It can take you to them. If you believe, you can talk to our ancestors on the trail of smoke. If you need them, call them. They will descend on the smoke trail to comfort you."*

Those words fired my imagination. I could picture the very ancestors that she had been telling me about—my Great-Grandmother Emma Brackette, her husband, Eli, Australia Brackette, who was nicked named Mink (she became the matriarch of the family after Emma died), Sis, Dewy, Bunk, Bo, Bud, Percy, and many other relatives, including her brother and sisters. Some were still alive. Others had gone on to live along the Milky Way.

I had heard my mother talk about those people with her brother Dick and sisters Emmie and Annie. They were family members who played critical roles in her life. Now she was talking to me about them. With the story about the trail of smoke that connected us, my ancestors seemed more real. I was so excited to learn about them!

At that time, in school, we were studying American Indian Chiefs. That evening, I asked my mother, *"If I wanted to communicate with my ancestors in the Milky Way, who would be their chief? Maybe I should communicate with the Chief if I have a big problem."*

I asked that question not to learn but instead because I was a smart-aleck kid. My mother did not pause to think about an answer. She replied to my question with total confidence, *"Tecumseh, the great Chief Tecumseh!"*

With that single name, my belief in my mother's stories about her Alabama Muscogee Creek Indian childhood faded. We had been taught, and I had read about the great Chief Tecumseh. He was not a Creek Indian. He was a Shawnee. The Shawnee were a northern tribe that lived in the Ohio River Valley near the Great Lakes, a thousand miles from the Creek tribe's homeland in southern Alabama's gently rolling red hills.

On that day, I was hurt to the quick. How could my mother have been so wrong? Those stories that had once intrigued me now seemed so fake, so fallacious, and made-up. I stopped listening to my mother's stories.

Much later, perhaps in college, I saw a book about Tecumseh. I leafed through it and was amazed. The Shawnee indeed lived in the Ohio River Valley, but in the 17th century Beaver War, a New York tribe, the Iroquois, armed with guns from their Dutch and British fur trading partners, began to move west to secure new hunting grounds.

The Iroquois had overhunted and depleted the fur-bearing animals in their traditional hunting grounds. Their neighbor tribes, armed with bows, arrows, and war clubs, were no match for the well-armed Iroquois with thunder sticks that spat smoke, fire, and death. Several tribes were slaughtered as the Iroquois moved west.

The Shawnee, having seen neighboring tribes massacred by Iroquois thunders sticks, left their Great Lakes homeland and traveled to Alabama, one thousand miles south of Ohio. During the Shawnee exile in Alabama, one of the Shawnee chiefs, named Puckshinwah (meaning alights from flying), married a Creek woman named Methotaske (meaning Turtle Laying Eggs in the Sand).

Puckshinwah ended the Shawnee exile and returned the tribe to Ohio. When they returned to the Ohio Valley, Methotaske gave birth to a son whom they named Tecumseh (literal meaning - Panther Passing Across, symbolic meaning, Blazing Comet).

Tecumseh was born in the heart of the Shawnee homeland. His father was a Shawnee chief. However, Creek Indians track lineage matrilineally. Because Tecumseh's mother was Creek, for Native Americans Tecumseh was also Creek, not Shawnee. Western historians portray Tecumseh as a Shawnee because they track lineage through the father.

I realized that all those years ago, my mother was right about Tecumseh. For her, in the matrilineal Native American tradition, Tecumseh was Creek!

How silly I felt. How foolish. Fortunately, my mother was still alive. I had the chance to make amends, to apologize to her for my childish foolishness. I did. My mother accepted my apology. That took a huge burden off my shoulders.

My mother knew that Tecumseh was a Creek Chief, but she did not know the rest of the story. She was not aware of the Shawnee move from Ohio to Alabama. She had never heard Tecumseh's father's and mother's names. She did not realize that Tecumseh's mother, Methotaske, was of the turtle clan. That was all new news for her.

When I told her the story, she said with great pride in her voice, *"Then WE - you and I - are of the same clan as Tecumseh!"* She was right. The clan may not be blood relatives, but it is the next closest thing. The clan is family!

I had often thought, *"If I could only go back in time to that first-grade class at Alabama Street School, I would do so on that embarrassing day when I was asked to talk about my heritage. My attitude would be different now with my more robust knowledge of my heritage."*

With pride on my face and in my voice, I would have loudly and boldly proclaimed my heritage to that class.

But, of course, we cannot time travel.

POSTSCRIPT

Tecumseh was incensed that white settlers were moving into the Midwest, taking the Indian homeland by force or trickery. He began to organize his Shawnee nation and other Indian tribes to protest and fight against American westward expansion.

A great orator, Tecumseh traveled extensively to other Indian nations, saying to them, *"A single twig breaks, but the bundle of twigs is strong."*

His message was harsh against Indian tribes ceding or selling their land to white settlers and against the American settler movement into Indian territory. Following is a quintessential Tecumseh quote. It is an exert from Tecumseh's speech to William Henry Harrison, circa 1810, delivered in Vincennes, Indian Territory:

"No tribe has the right to sell, even to each other, much less to strangers... Sell a country! Why not sell the air, the great sea, as well as the earth? Didn't the Great Spirit make them all for the use of his children?"

"The way, the only way to stop this evil (white settlers moving onto traditional Indian tribal lands) is for the red man to unite in claiming a common and equal right in the land, as it was first, and should be now, for it was never divided.

We gave them forest-clad mountains and valleys full of game, and in return, what did they give our warriors and our women? Rum, trinkets, and a grave."~ Tecumseh

A 1763 British government proclamation designated all the land between the Appalachian Mountains and the Mississippi River as Indian Territory. After winning the Revolutionary War, America was lax in enforcing the British proclamation and began to encourage Americans to expand westward and settle on what had been Indian land.

In the lead-up to the War of 1812, the British promised Tecumseh that if he allied with the British, Britain would strictly enforce the 1763 Proclamation. With America's defeat, the British promised Tecumseh a vast Indian Territory "off limits" to American settlers. That promise was well worth fighting for, so Tecumseh formally allied his Indian Confederacy with the British.

In 1811, to expand his confederacy, Tecumseh traveled from Ohio to his mother's homeland – Alabama. There, he met with the Creek, Chickasaw, Choctaw, Seminole, and Cherokee nations to recruit them to fight with him as members of his confederacy. Tecumseh told the gathered Indian chiefs that the Great Spirit would turn the world dark and shake the earth to support his call to war. An eclipse darkened the sky; an earthquake shook Indian teepees across the homelands of the 5 Civilized Tribes, and some, including the Red Stick faction of the Creek nation, sided with Britain against America as members of Tecumseh's confederacy.

It was a troubled time. On June 1, 1812, the U.S. Congress formally declared war on Great Britain (the War of 1812). Tecumseh and his growing Indian confederacy fought against the American army in the North, and his allies, the Red Stick Creek, fought against American settlers and the army in the South.

In the North, Tecumseh's warriors engaged in brutal battles against Major General William Henry Harrison. Battles were fought in Ohio, Indiana, Michigan, and in what is now Ontario, Canada.

In 1813, 500 of Tecumseh's warriors, led by Tecumseh, were at the Thames River in Canada waiting for British reinforcements. Before the British reinforcement troops arrived, a 3,500-man American force attacked Tecumseh's much smaller fighting force.

Tecumseh's army was decimated by the much larger and better-armed American army. On October 5, 1813, Tecumseh was killed on the Thames River battlefield. Tecumseh died in the same way he often told his men they should die, *"When our time comes to die... sing your death song and die like a hero going home."*

In August 1813, at Fort Mims, some 40 miles north of Mobile, Alabama, Red Stick Creek warriors attacked the fortified homestead, defeated the defending militia, and then slaughtered the remaining men, women, and children. In retaliation, in March 1814, General Andrew Jackson led a military force of almost 3,000 Americans, strengthened by Cherokee and White Stick Creek warriors, against Red Stick warriors at a fortified area on the Tallapoosa River in Central Alabama. The Red Stick army was annihilated. Some 800 Red Stick warriors were killed.

After his death, Tecumseh's Indian confederacy fell apart. The Red Stick defeat and Britain's defeat by General Andrew Jackson at the Battle of New Orleans ended the War of 1812, as did the hopes for a vast Indian-only settler—free territory stretching from the Appalachian Mountains to the Mississippi River.

It was the end of an era and far worse. The victorious American administration passed severe measures against the southeastern Indian tribes. On May 28, 1830, President Andrew Jackson signed the infamous Indian Removal Act. From 1830 to 1850, the U.S. Government seized millions of acres of Indian tribal homelands in Alabama, Georgia, Tennessee, North Carolina, and Florida, impacting one hundred fifty thousand tribal people. 100,000 Creek, Chickasaw, Choctaw, Seminole, and Cherokee men, women, and children were force-marched to a desolate territory west of the Mississippi River.

An estimated 15,000 Indian men, women, and children died on "Nunahi-Duna-Dlo-Hilu-I" (Trail Where They Cried) - The Trail of Tears. The Indian Removal Act is now remembered as a "Journey of Injustice". It is one of the darkest chapters in American history.

The Brackette family avoided being removed from Alabama to Oklahoma by hiding in the forest. As outlaws, they could not own land. They survived as sharecroppers, working the land of others. Understandably, Brackette ancestors seldom talked about their lives and times. When they did, it was in whispers at night after the kids were asleep, so their history and stories, ways and traditions have been lost and forgotten.

This book shares personal stories from my childhood and family stories remembered by my mother, which I pieced together as best I could. It is written to preserve and share family memories at the request of some younger Brackette descendants.

They wanted to know more about our family's Native American heritage because there are many versions. Some claim our family is Cherokee or Choctaw. My mother was a family matriarch for many years. She was sure about our Creek heritage. I realize she represents one person's opinion, but I trust and believe her.

I welcome comments and corrections to what I've written. I have done my best with my mother's memories, and I will do so with anything else shared with me.

A simple genealogical chart follows of our Brackette family.

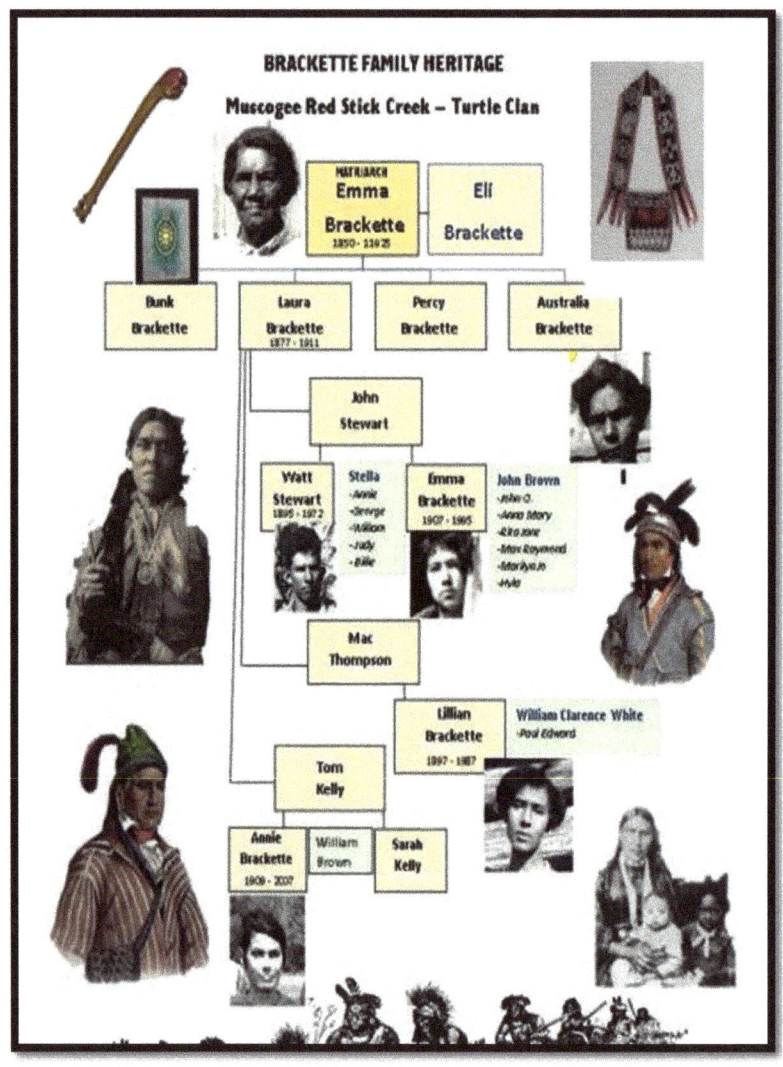

BRACKETTE FAMILY HERITAGE

Muscogee Red Stick Creek – Turtle Clan

Emma and Lillian Olivia Brackette, Muskogee Creek,
Circa 1915

Emmie, Annie, Bay, Mink, Emma, and Pete, circa 1915

BLUE THISTLE

Some months ago, at a Toastmasters meeting, I was asked, *"How did you become such a creative fellow?"* I stuttered and stammered my way through that very personal question. I didn't answer it very well. On the way home from that meeting, I asked myself, *"How might I have better responded to that personal question?"*

Nothing came to mind. Late that evening, in the quiet time before sleep came, I found myself slipping into a dream-like reverie. In that very relaxed state, an image of my long-departed mother shimmered into view. She smiled at a very young boy and taught him an important lesson. The boy had his back to me. When he turned around, I saw that the boy was me.

My Creek Indian mother was the very best teacher I ever had. Because she only had a second-grade education, she did not teach me book learning. Instead, she shared with me sacred Creek Indian shaman secrets passed from generation to generation through whispered stories around flickering Muskogee Creek tribal campfires.

In my reverie, my mother's melodious voice was saying, *"Little Paul - when you have a problem in life, a question that needs an answer, if I am not with you"* (and she no longer is), *"look to Nature. Everything you will ever need to know can be found floating on a soft summer breeze, heard in the light pitter-patter of falling rain, seen in the glistening smallness of a dew drop, or the sky-filling grandeur of a fiery sunset. Watch and listen, Little Paul, and heed Nature's subtle yet powerful messages. Nature will never deceive you."*

With those prophetic words, my mother's image faded from the reverie and was replaced by an almost psychedelic blue-green object - a blue thistle plant. How strange was that thistle image?

I grew up in southern Indiana farm country, so I knew that thistle is a pesky plant reviled by farmers. Its prickly thorns enjoy drawing blood from hands or legs with just a casual touch. Thistle is a money-stealing invasive plant that competes with corn, wheat, and other cash crops.

Why was a blue thistle plant making an appearance in my reverie? That pondering pushed me even deeper into the dream-like trance. My relaxed mind recalled a long-forgotten connection– a passing love affair with blue thistle.

In the 1940s, things were more straightforward than they are now. As a boy, I could freely explore the world around me without worry. Leaving my home on a summer's day on my Schwinn bicycle, I could head for an unknown destination. Seldom would my mother ask where I was going. If she did, she did not need a specific location.

I could say, *"I'm going down a country road north of town."* That was OK with her, but as I rode away, Mother always said, *"Remember, be home before dark."*

One lazy, hazy southern Indiana summer day, far from my home on North Columbia Street, I was on a hilly, winding dirt road. In the day's heat, a colossal oak tree shouted at me, *"Hey, little boy, stop! Put your bike in my shade. Come. Climb me. Enjoy the beautiful view."*

When I climbed the oak tree, my world went from mundane to magical. From a high limb, I saw a most beautiful woodland meadow. It was hypnotically blue—a field of blue thistle. Once, it had probably been a cornfield, but now the blue thistle had taken over. That made no difference to me. It was the most beautiful sight I had ever seen.

From high in the oak tree, the field looked like a vast ocean -- in landlocked southern Indiana. I was a thousand miles from the Atlantic Ocean and two thousand miles from the Pacific Ocean, but I had discovered an ocean just a bike ride from my home in Brazil, Indiana.

The reverie empowered my mind to make connections - to connect dots. The blue thistle ocean was one long-forgotten "dot" in my young life. Now that the memory had been stirred, more memories about this blue thistle ocean began to flood my thoughts.

I visited my thistle ocean many times during that lost-in-time and memory summer some 70 years ago. I remember how I felt when I first saw the blue thistle ocean. In my boyish mind, I was transported from Indiana to places distant in time and space.

Looking at the blue thistle ocean from the boughs of the oak tree, I was no longer a small boy in Indiana. I became a clipper ship captain, sailing my ship on uncharted blue seas at an exciting time in history – the Age of Exploration and Discovery.

From my perch high in that old oak tree, I could feel my imaginary clipper ship pitch and roll as it rose and fell on powerful ocean currents. I could watch the wind fill my ship's sails. I could smell the salty sea water as it splashed on my face. I could hear the poignant cry of seagulls high above my clipper ship in a bluer-than-blue sky.

On a stormy Indiana day, the thistle would bend and bow to an angry north wind. As it did, the thistle looked like undulating waves. It would take all my strength to man the helm of the clipper ship. I could imagine that I was sailing in the turbulent waters of the Cape of Good Hope.

On a quiet Indiana day, the thistle would go motionless. My clipper ship would be stuck in the stifling heat and stagnant, unmoving water of a sea that the Ancient Mariner called the Doldrums. Would the boat ever sail beyond this quiescent sea?

High in that oak tree, I could be Christopher Columbus sailing for Queen Isabella of Castile to discover a New World. Or I could be Ferdinand Magellan circumnavigating the globe for King Charles the First. Or I could be Sir Francis Drake on the Golden Hind sailing around South America for Queen Elizabeth the First. I also could be Blackbeard or Captain Morgan, both pirates who looted and plundered their way through the pearly waters of the Caribbean.

I woke from that reverie, realizing that my brain had taken me into its hidden recesses to find the answer I had been searching for - how I had developed a powerful imagination. One answer was that long-forgotten meadow - my blue thistle ocean. It was a deep wellspring that contributed to the development of my creativity.

In that oak tree, I was free, without judgment, to become anyone I wanted to be and to travel anywhere in time and space. My only limit was my imagination.

My mother was right when she said, *"Mother Nature will never deceive you."* My mind took me to Nature -- to the oak tree and the blue thistle field of my childhood. It unlocked a treasure trove of long-forgotten memories that significantly impacted my development. I awoke with a better understanding of who I am and why I am the way I am.

Toastmasters founder Dr. Ralph Smedley once said, *"Toastmasters is, first of all, a voyage of self-discovery."* Thanks to Dr. Smedley and Toastmasters, I continue to mine my past experiences by recalling and connecting dots in a passionate journey of rich personal exploration and deep and satisfying self-discovery.

Have you ever looked back and connected your remembered and sometimes long-forgotten dots? If not, perhaps you should. You will learn about yourself in exciting new ways. You will savor delicious old wines in new bottles and discover a "one-in-the-universe" unique world that only you can explore. I call that extremely personal world the world of "YOU."

"You will never regret going to YOUR WORLD!

WITCHES

I was six years old in 1947. It might be hard for you to picture ancient, decrepit me as a six-year-old boy, but I assure you that once upon a time—long, long ago—I was a six-year-old. And I already had a first love.

No, not what you think. My first love was......my Schwinn bicycle. When I was on my bike, under an open sky, with the wind in my face, and using my imagination, I could be anyone, anywhere.

I could be a clipper ship captain circumnavigating the globe. I could be a space cadet on a secret spy mission out beyond the rings of Saturn. Or I could be a Shoshone Indian warrior on a magnificent steed galloping across a beautiful purple-sage plain.

As expansive as my imaginary universe was, my real world was greatly circumscribed by my mother's rules about where I could ride my bicycle when I was first learning to ride it.

I could not take my bike from my driveway onto Columbia Street. I remember my mother's words – *Little Paul, never ever ride your bicycle in the street. Only on the sidewalk!"*

On the sidewalk, I was not permitted to turn to the left. A hazardous street, Hendrix Street, was just a few houses away. In the 1940s, cars on Hendrix Street might be speeding as fast as 8 or 10 miles an hour! How dangerous was that!

There were also rules about turning to the right. My mother would shake her finger at me and say, *"Little Paul, NEVER EVER go any further than the Woodall house."* The Woodall house was only three houses away from my house -- the White House.

Friday, Oct 30th, 1947, was Halloween eve. It was a beautiful fall day in Brazil, Indiana. The sky was a deep cerulean blue, a sure harbinger of a cold winter yet to come. From His expansive palette, God had imbued the autumn leaves with dazzling red, orange, and gold hues. In their brilliance, the leaves were playfully dancing to the gentle caress of a light autumnal breeze.

The pungent smell of burnt leaves from last night's bonfire still lingered in the crisp air and teased my nose. Excitedly, I climbed on my bike and headed down my driveway to Columbia Street. At Columbia Street, I turned to the right because I always tried to be an obedient child. I pedaled hard in front of the Oliver house. By the Armstrong house, I was moving at full speed. Then, all too soon, I was in front of the Woodall house.

On that beautiful autumn day, I put my head down, pedaled hard, and zipped past the Woodall house into unexplored territory. I was by a cornfield. I saw faded yellow corn stalks, withered by an early frost, and huge orange pumpkins. Tied together at the top, the corn stalks looked like American Indian teepees.

I shifted my gaze back to Columbia Street. That was when I saw it! I saw the biggest, blackest car I had ever seen. It turned onto Columbia Street from Midland Street. That big car stopped about 50 yards from where I was. The car door opened. Three women, dressed in black from head to toe, got out of the car.

I pumped my bicycle brakes. My bike screeched to a stop almost directly across Columbia Street from the three women. I watched as they seemed to float around their car. They floated up onto the sidewalk. Then they floated up onto the front porch of the house I knew as the Deal house because the Deal family lived there.

My eyes were as big as saucers. My heart was pounding. My mind was screaming, *"Those three women - they're HALLOWEEN WITCHES!"*

The front door of the Deal house opened. The first two witches floated into the Deal house. The third was the oldest and ugliest of the three witches. She had a huge hook nose, pale blueish skin, and a face full of wrinkles. The ugly old witch started into the house, but then she stopped, turned, and stared right at me with tiny, beady witch eyes.

The old witch began to raise her right hand slowly. Some say what happened next was just my boyish imagination. I'll let you be the judge. I saw a brilliant flash of fire shoot from the palm of the old witch's hand. A flaming ball of fire streaked across Columbia Street. It hit my chest, knocking me off my bicycle. *OUCH,"* I cried as my knee hit an unforgiving sidewalk. *"OUUUF,"* I grunted as my bike fell on top of me.

I was in great pain! My right knee was split open. Blood was everywhere! As I looked at the blood gushing from my knee, a warm, wet spot began to form on the front of my pants. I knew I was in DEEP doo-doo. I had disobeyed my mother, torn my pants, bloodied my knee, and worse yet, I had wet my pants!

My mind was racing. Dilly-dally was not an option. What if those witches were to reappear? I knew that things were often worse the second time around. I had to act now.

I stood on a painful right leg and turned my bike toward home. As I got on the bike, my sore knee impeded my motion, and unknown to me, my foot hit the bicycle's chain, knocking it off its sprocket. Unaware of that, I pedaled as hard and fast as I could. The pedals spun like crazy, but the chainless bike was not moving. The harder I pedaled, the more the bike just stood still. My mind screamed out, *"It's a WITCH's SPELL!"*

I threw that bewitched bicycle down. I ran toward the White House as fast as possible on an injured leg. At the Woodall house, I looked up. Through tear-filled eyes, I saw my mother standing in front of my house, arms akimbo, and with a switch in her hand. That raised a question in my mind. *"How do mothers know?"*

But my mother could see I was in trouble. She ran to me as I was running to her. Mother took me in her arms, looked me over, and asked, *"Little Paul, are you OK?"*

She must have decided that I was OK because a Grand Inquisition ensued. *"What happened? Where's your bike? Why are your pants torn? Why is your knee bloody? Did you.... WET your pants?"*

All I could muster was – *"Mommy – there are witches down there at the Deal house!"*

"Little Paul, let's go find your bike." My mother took my hand and walked me closer to the Deal house. As we approached the bike,

the front door of the Deal house opened. The three awful witches floated out onto the porch. The oldest witch stepped in front of the other two.

When the old witch slowly raised her right hand, I hid behind my mother's dress. From that sheltered place, I looked at my mother. She seemed so brave and undisturbed by what was going on.

Then I heard the old witch cackle and say in a screechy witch's voice – *"Lillian, is that your son?"* As I tried to understand why that witch knew my mother's name, my mother did the unthinkable. She jerked me from behind her dress, putting me in harm's way. Then she replied sweetly, *"Yes, this is my little man. This is little Paul."*

My mother not only put me in harm's way, she told those witches my name. I was confused, not knowing what to think. I expected the worst, but nothing happened.

The witches floated around their big black car, got in, and as they drove away, they all waved goodbye. My mother smiled at the witches, waved goodbye, and then took my hand and forced me to wave goodbye to them. *"Was my mother in cahoots with a coven of witches?"*

Thanks to my Halloween Eve bike ride out beyond the Woodall house, in clear violation of my mother's rules, I learned three valuable life lessons. First, children should always obey their parents. The rules are there for a reason.

Second, I learned that my imagination could quickly get me into trouble. It did on that day! Over 70 years later, my imagination still gets me in trouble. Just this morning – but that is a tale for another day.

The third lesson was the most important. On that October day in 1947, on Halloween eve, in Brazil, Indiana, I learned all about.... religion! Those three women, dressed in black from head to toe, were not Halloween witches. They were CATHOLIC NUNS!

I had never seen a Catholic nun before. But on that October day, seeing those three nuns, I learned this valuable lesson that has helped me throughout the years:

"You cannot always judge a book by its cover, but you can always know a nun by her habit."

HELP ME MAKE IT THROUGH THE NIGHT

In late August 1966, I left my Indiana birthplace to become an International Voluntary Services (IVS) English language teacher in Laos. Starting something new is often difficult. The International Voluntary Services adventure in Laos was problematic, dangerous, and sometimes terrifying. But it was also amazingly wonderful in more ways than I can count.

My high school geography teacher could not find Laos on a map, but I soon learned firsthand where it was. It took an epic 60-hour airplane journey to reach Laos. From Indianapolis, just 60 miles from my home in Brazil, Indiana, I flew to Chicago, Denver, San Francisco, Honolulu, Tokyo, Hong Kong, Saigon, and Bangkok before finally arriving in Vientiane, Laos, the capital city of the Kingdom of a Million Elephants.

Reaching Vientiane, I still had miles to go before arriving at my ultimate destination – the valley of Sam Thong, located in Xieng Khouang Province, in northeast Laos, near the border with North Vietnam. Sam Thong was 200 miles from Vientiane and could only be reached by helicopter or short take-off landing (STOL) aircraft. I had no idea about the adventures that awaited me there.

Sam Thong was in the heartland of one of Laos' many ethnic minorities - a hill tribe -- the Hmong. The Hmong people lived much as they had thousands of years ago. Other than the two adjacent valleys of Sam Thong and Long Tieng, there was no electric grid in the Hmong homeland, no roads, and no running water – which, among other things, meant no flush toilets. The Hmong homeland was among the most primitive places on earth. While I didn't know it at the time, the Hmong paramilitary or guerrilla army under General Vang Pao, supported by America's Central Intelligence Agency (CIA), was an important element of America's Vietnam War strategy. The Hmong greatly appreciated U.S. support as it enabled them to defend their homeland from North Vietnamese communist occupation. At the same time, the securing of a viable buffer zone between increasingly communist Vietnam and democratically free Thailand was a key U.S. objective in the hottest part of the Cold War.

China and Russia supported North Vietnam's war machine. The Ho Chi Minh Trail ran through the Hmong homeland in Laos and was communist North Vietnam's main supply route for moving war material and communist troops to support their brutal insurgency in South Vietnam. The Trail was a high-priority military target for the U.S. in the Vietnam War.

The U.S. Government supported South Vietnam's government with a significant American military presence. Laos had no sizeable military presence, but the U.S. supported the Royal Lao government's army and a Neutral force. In addition, in what was called its "Secret War," the CIA supported special guerilla units in their battle against communist aggression. In northeast Laos' Military Region II, the CIA supported the Hmong army led by General Vang Pao.

In northeast Laos, communist forces operated from a geographic stronghold called the Plain of Jars to the north of the Sam Thong and Long Tieng valleys. General Vang Pao's Hmong army of anti-communist guerrilla fighters was based in the Long Tieng valley.

I was assigned to teach English in Sam Thong, just over a mountain ridge from Long Tieng. Just as Long Tieng served as the headquarters for military operations in northeast Laos, Sam Thong was the headquarters for the Xieng Khouang Provincial government's civilian and humanitarian operations. The Governor's office was in Sam Thong, as were the offices of the Superintendent of Schools. I taught English to Hmong teachers at a French-system Teacher Training Institute (ENI). I also taught English to Hmong nurses and medics at the Xieng Khouang Provincial Hospital.

I was generally aware that northeast Laos was a war zone. Still, I had no idea, until I arrived there, how complicated the war was and how much it dominated everything that happened in the Hmong homeland. I quickly learned that I was living and working in a red-hot war zone.

The final 200-mile flight from Vientiane to Sam Thong was made in a tiny airplane that had room for only a pilot and co-pilot. At the military side of Vientiane's airport, a grizzled American pilot looked down at me from his small single-engine aircraft, *"Hey there - I'm Jim. Are you the new Sam Thong teacher? Climb aboard."*

Summoning courage, I climbed up to the co-pilot's seat. The engine roared, and the short take-off/landing plane taxied a few feet and seemed to jump into the air. Once airborne, the small plane bumped and bounced on the turbulent air currents from Laos' mountainous terrain. I had never experienced anything like that before. I was Black, with the last name White, but I was turning Green from the turbulence.

"Hang on a little longer, son; we are almost there." After one hour of bouncing, rocking, and rolling, Pilot Jim said, *"Look down at that green valley, son. That's your new home - Sam Thong."*

A long dirt airstrip was nestled between two mountains. There was a western building at one end of the airstrip. A dozen airplanes and helicopters were parked near that building. Scattered over the rest of the valley were many bamboo and thatch huts. A few had tin roofs.

"GET READY," I'm gonna take her down."*

The plane fell from the sky in tight spirals and slammed onto the runway.

"So sorry, son. That's called a corkscrew—no gliding landing up here. We're in a war zone. BAD GUYS could be on top of them there mountains. I corkscrewed because otherwise, we might get the SUGAR shot out of us."

As the plane taxied down the airstrip, I took a deep breath and said, *"Paul, what have you gotten yourself into?"*

The airplane's radio screeched, *"Jim - this here is Pop. Is that schoolteacher on board?"* *"Yes, sir."*

"Drop him at the FAR end of the airstrip."

"That's a Charlie-Charlie," Jim replied, *"Correct - will do."*

Jim taxied his plane to the far end of the airstrip. He stopped and said, *"End of the line, son. Jump out."* Jim waved and shouted at

65

me, *"Watch out for the bad guys; remember, some good guys might be bad guys.*

Son...never forget, this here is a WAR ZONE."

Jim turned the plane and taxied away, leaving me in a thick cloud of red dust from his propeller. The dust choked me. When the dust cleared, and I stopped coughing, I looked around for my welcoming party. There was none. I was standing by my lonesome with just my backpack – on a red laterite dirt airstrip in the middle of nowhere. I was in a strange land, half a world away from my family and all I knew and held dear.

Thinking about what Jim said, I thought, "I'd be happy to see any guy right now – good *or bad."* I felt abandoned and helpless. I didn't know what to do.

I waited for what seemed like an eternity. Not one soul came to greet me. I could see activity at the Western-style building. I decided to walk to the other end of the airstrip, but as I picked up my backpack, I saw a green jeep turn and head toward me. Soon, the jeep skidded to a stop right before me, enveloping me in another cloud of choking red laterite dust. The driver was an elderly American man with a cigarette hanging from his bottom lip. He leaned from the jeep and growled at me, *"You the new teacher?"*

"Yes, I....."

"I'm Pop Buell. I run this here operation." He pointed. *"See them there buildings over yonder cross the valley?"*

"Yes, I...." Pop interrupted me again. *"That's the school. That's where YOU belong. That trail at your feet – it'll take you there. NOW, listen up. About this airstrip- things go on up here that you DON'T want to see and DON'T want to know. Just get your black butt* -- (he was more explicit than that) -- *over to the school and keep it over there. Don't ever let me catch you up here on this airstrip. Do you understand?"*

Before I could respond, and with those warm words of welcome ringing in my ears, the man called "Pop" drove away, leaving me in

66

another cloud of red laterite dust. When I quit coughing, it seemed I had no choice. I dusted myself off, picked up my backpack, and walked down the trail, thinking, *"Paul, why are you here? What have you gotten yourself into?"*

The trail led to a small open-air market on the floor of the broad valley. Thirty or forty men, women, and children milled around a dozen women who sat on dirty blankets selling food.

This was my first encounter with the Hmong. The men wore black Chinese-style pajamas. The women had more style. Their skirts were decorated with colorful, intricate embroidery. Some wore what seemed like heavy silver necklaces. The children were as naked as jaybirds.

The strange, pungent smells of that market were not pleasing. Exotic fruit and unknown food were spread out on blankets on the ground. One woman was selling bloody chunks of fly-covered meat.

I felt like throwing up. But two things were even more disturbing than what I was looking at. First, all the men and most of the women carried rifles. Many Hmong in that market carried the most enormous knives I had ever seen. The pilot's words *'WAR ZONE'* took on more immediacy for me.

Second, and even more frightening, was the way the Hmong reacted to me. I didn't see one smile. There was not one pro-offered handshake or friendly gesture. The eyes of the Hmong at that market seemed cold and vacant.

I felt like an interloper in their world. The pilot's words returned to me: *"This Sam Thong Valley is your new home."*

That Hmong market in the Sam Thong Valley was like a surrealistic painting – and I was in it. Fear overpowered me. I couldn't breathe. I ran from the marketplace and did not stop until I was on the school grounds.

Another surprise awaited me at the school. There were several empty buildings, but where were the students? Where were the teachers? Where was the welcoming party? *"Paul, what have you gotten yourself into?"*

I sat on the wooden steps of one of the buildings, wondering what to do next. I knew I'd better heed Pop's warning by not returning to the airstrip, but there didn't seem to be any other option.

After another stress-filled eternity, I saw a small boy walking toward me. He motioned with his hand for me to follow him, which I did. He led me to a tiny thatch hut on high stilts. The boy signaled for me to climb the rickety bamboo railing to the hut's front door - a jagged hole hacked into the hut's bamboo siding.

I cautiously climbed the bamboo railing. I wasn't sure it would hold my weight, but it did. At the top, I turned to thank the boy and see what else he had for me. The boy was nowhere in sight. He had disappeared.

I peered into the bamboo hut. Its one room had no furniture on its woven bamboo floor. The window was a hole crudely hacked in the wall by one of those knives I saw at the market. I felt lost. I felt sick. I asked myself, *"Paul, what have you got yourself into?"*

From the window, I looked out at a beautiful sight. The broad Sam Thong valley stretched from the school to the market to the airstrip. Beyond the airstrip were green mountains, a strikingly blue sky, and white billowing clouds. It was like a picture postcard. I smiled and relaxed for the first time since arriving in Sam Thong.

I enjoyed watching the sun fall behind the green mountains. Then, there was another surprise. There was no evening, twilight, or sunset. The sun was gone in a nanosecond, and the valley went from glorious light to an all-encompassing pitch-black darkness.

It was so dark that I could not see my hand in front of my face. The hut did not have electricity. I could see a faint glow of lights at the distant airstrip, but otherwise, everything was blacker than black. For the first time in my life, I could not simply flip a switch and turn on a light. I started to panic.

I didn't smoke, so I didn't have matches or a cigarette lighter. I had no way to drive away the darkness that had enveloped me. As I stood in the darkness of the hut, hyperventilating, I wanted to scream.

But before I could, I had another frightening surprise. A brilliant star appeared at the valley's far end. It was high in the black night sky. The bright light was hypnotic. Then, a second star appeared. Then, a third. Next, I heard a dull thudding sound – *"whump - whump."* Pilot Jim's words came to my mind again – *"Son, it's a WAR ZONE!"*

I thought, *"The sound must be artillery fire or mortars. The bright stars must be military flares. Are we being attacked by the North Vietnamese communists?"*

Fear gripped me. I wanted to run, but where could I run in this dark, unknown place? *"Paul, what have you got yourself into?"*

All I could do was stand at the window and watch. Soon, I was looking at a dozen bright lights snaking their way high in the night sky. They would come in and then fall out of view. Panic spurred my mind to work. I had an ah-ha moment – *"These aren't mortars or flares. From their movement, they must be flaming torches being carried down a mountain path by villagers."*

That would account for their snaking motion and coming into and out of sight. But what about the sound? *"Perhaps a drum. Perhaps villagers were walking down a trail while beating drums.*

Those were comforting thoughts. Perhaps we were not under North Vietnamese attack. No longer afraid, I stretched my tired body onto the hut's bamboo floor, hoping to sleep. I thought, *"Tomorrow will have to be a better day."*

I closed my eyes and perhaps slept a little. But soon, I was jolted to my feet by a thunderous sound! It was so loud that it shook the hut – *" WHUMP!"*

Shaking again, I stood up and looked out of the window. I could barely stand on weak legs. I couldn't catch my breath. I was hyperventilating again. As I gasped for air, sweat poured down my forehead and into my eyes. I had goose pimples. My arm hair stood on end.

The drum sound shook my very being. Then, I heard a human-wailing sound between drumbeats. It was unlike anything I had ever heard. And I could now see the drummers and wailers. I watched them with fear. They were carrying flaming torches that cast flickering light on their faces. Their wails sounded like utterances by banshees from the hottest part of hell. *"WHUMP, WHOOWHOOOO, WHUMP, WHOWHOOOO!"*

My heart raced. I thought, *"Did I violate a Hmong cultural norm at the market? Did seeing my dark face cause a child to fall ill or die? Did a woman abort after seeing me? Were the Hmong coming to exact revenge on me for some tragedy that had befallen them?"*

I could now clearly see the Hmong men. They were circling my hut in ever tighter circles. Their faces were taught and angry.

Their eyes were cold. Glistening in the torchlight, I could see tears on their cheeks. *"Were these deranged opium-addicted Hmong Ku Klux Klansmen? Were they going to burn the hut down with me in it? Were they going to hack my body into bloody chunks of meat with those huge knives?*

"Would I die on this very night, in this bamboo hut, half a world away from everyone I knew? Would my parents ever know what happened to me?

Illuminated by the flickering light of their torches, I saw sweaty, distorted faces. Tear-filled, cold, angry eyes stared at me.

Otherworldly wails shook the depth of me, as did the slow, penetrating dirge beat of the drums. Faces contorted with anger and twisted with hate were fixed on me.

"Paul, "Why are you here? What have you gotten yourself into?"

In desperation, I found religion. I heard myself uttering an anguished prayer – *"Father in Heaven – God - please, please, please help me make it through the night."*

Perhaps from fear or exhaustion, my prayers seemed to be answered. I strangely found solace. My world started to spin out of control. My legs grew weak. I fell to the bamboo floor, unconscious.

The next thing I recall was a feeling that something was tickling my face. I slowly opened my eyes and moved my hands to my face. A beam of warm sunlight came through a crack in the bamboo wall and played on my face. The sunbeam's dance had awakened me.

I sat up. It was daylight! I quickly felt my body with my hands. I was thankful to God that I was still in one piece. The knives had not hacked me into bloody chunks of meat.

God had answered my prayers. He had helped me through that night of terror. I thought, *"Was last night just a dreadful nightmare?"*

Outside the hut, in the bright light of day, I saw hundreds of footprints in the dirt circling the hut. I could smell the kerosene from fiery torches. Cigarette buts and other debris were scattered around. It was not a nightmare. Men had circled the hut.

"But why? What had I done to deserve that terror?"

I walked to the school. Kids were playing in the schoolyard. Several teachers came to greet me. One spoke a little English. He apologized to me, *"So solly Mr. White, Yesterday we no meet you at airport or at school. All Sam Thong at hospital."*

"Communist kill Hmong pilot. Shoot his airplane. Plane crash. Burn. Hmong pilot dead. Last night, we carry dead pilot body from airstrip to his hut. All villagers come to mourn. Pilot's hut behind your hut. All night, we mourn dead pilot."

Now I knew the rest of the story. The drums, the torches, the gut-wrenching wails – had nothing to do with me. The Hmong were not opium-addicted Klansmen seeking brutal revenge. They did not circle my hut to hack my body to pieces with their knives for something I had done. They were mourning a fallen war hero.

On that fiery night of terror, I discovered I was carrying a heavy load of mental baggage. I learned that dropping heavy baggage frees our hands, which, in turn, frees our hearts and minds. That freedom enables us to better understand the world around us.

We all carry mental baggage. If we could just identify and let go of our mental baggage, what a wonderful world this would be!

LS 20 (Sam Thong) airstrip, circa 1967

Tan Pop (Edgar Buell), Indiana Farmer at a Sam Thong
ceremony, circa 1967

Paul E. White, IVS Volunteer at the ENI Sam Thong,
circa 1966

General Vang Pao and Paul E. White, Wisconsin
Hmong ceremony

Paul and Raven FAC, circa 1968

PEW Cold War Warrior, circa 1968

Knighting at the Royal Palace in Luang Prabang

Knighthood - Year of the Pig, 14th day of the rising moon

WHEN THE STUDENT IS READY

Ancient Chinese philosopher Lao Tzu wrote, *"When the student is ready, the teacher will appear."* We don't know in what form or who the teacher will be. Sometimes, it will be someone we never suspected could be our teacher.

The person who taught me the most about Cold War politics was not a pin-stripe suit-wearing internationally traveling diplomat at the State Department in Washington DC or a foreign service officer at a far-flung U.S. Embassy in Asia, Africa, or Europe. It was not a military camouflage field fatigue-wearing Special Forces Green Beret commander at the Fort Bragg Special Warfare School where I trained. It was an ethnic minority hill tribe Special Guerrilla Unit commander who had probably not even traveled beyond northeast Laos's misty mountains and high jungles.

I originally went to Laos to work in a refugee program for Hmong tribespeople who were being impacted by the buffer zone war in Laos associated with the Vietnam War. The Hmong were fierce warriors defending their homeland against North Vietnamese incursion. America's Central Intelligence Agency (CIA) provided a guerrilla army led by General Vang Pao with weapons, ammunition, supplies, training, air, and other support in what was dubbed the CIA's "Secret War" in Laos.

There is an old Southeast Asian adage, "When two elephants fight, the grass is trampled." The two Cold War elephants were

democracy, American style, and Russian and Chinese communism.

The Cold War elephant fights happened in many places around the world in proxy wars, including in Vietnam. Laos was a sideshow to the Vietnam War. In northeast Laos, the two Cold War elephants were fighting. The Hmong and other hill tribes were the grass being trampled.

After graduate school, I tried to find a job working with Hmong refugees in Thailand or Laos. I could not find such a job, so I reluctantly accepted a position with International Voluntary

Services (IVS) as a teacher in Laos. I was promised I would be posted in a valley in the heart of the Hmong homeland.

I was assigned to an ENI (a French education system Teacher Training Institute) in Sam Thong, Xieng Khoang Province. From the ENI, I could see the airstrip and the U.S. Agency for International Development's (USAID) refugee program I wanted to work in. However, Edgar "Pop" Buell, the USAID official who ran the refugee operation, had ordered me to do my job at the school and stay away from the refugee and war effort at Sam Thong's airstrip. As instructed, I learned Lao and basic Hmong and successfully found ways to contribute to education at the teacher training school. I stayed away from the airstrip.

At the school, I worked closely with Moua Lia, the Superintendent of Schools for Xieng Khouang and Sam Neua provinces, and with Chao Saykham, the Governor of Xieng Khouang Province. I gained the respect of these two civilian authorities.

One morning in January of 1967, "Pop" Buell drove across the Sam Thong Valley from the airstrip to the school in his green jeep. A heavy strain showed on Pop's grizzled face and in his posture. *"Paul, we just suffered a tragedy. Don Sjostrom, one of my key refugee operations officers, was killed by the North Vietnamese during a firefight at Lima Site 36, Na Khang. I urgently need an operations officer to step in and keep our operation staffed."*

"I know you have wanted to work in my refugee program. You've done a great job here at the school. Your Lao is good. The leaders and the teachers love your dedication, hard work, and willingness to contribute in any way you can. And you have followed my orders to stay away from the airstrip."

"If you are still interested, I'm offering you a provisional position at the airstrip in my refugee relief program." Pop added, *"The North Vietnamese are on a fierce offensive. Refugees are being generated all over northeast Laos.*

We are swamped. I need you, and I need your decision – now!"

I did not hesitate. *"Pop, I am sorry about Don. He was a good man. Teachers still remember him for the good work he did at the ENI. YES, I accept. I have long wanted to work as an operations officer. What must I do to move from the school to the airstrip operation?"*

Pop said, *"I have already talked to Moua Lia, Chao Saykham, and General Vang Pao (the Military Region II Hmong guerilla army leader). They all agree to my giving you a try. You don't need to do anything. They have no objections to your move from the ENI to the refugee program."*

We went to Pop's office, a Quonset hut at the airstrip. Pop told his secretary and radio operator, Carol Mills, *"Get Charlie Mann on the single sideband radio."* Charlie Mann was USAID/Laos' Mission Director based in the country's capital, Vientiane.

In the conversation, Pop revealed something I was not aware of. *"Charlie, you told me that an International Voluntary Services volunteer serving in a forward area was killed and that there has been pressure to move Paul from Sam Thong and to recall all IVS volunteers serving in forward-area assignments. I am calling to say that Paul doesn't want to be reassigned.*

Paul will stay in place here in Sam Thong. He will work for me in the refugee program. With the loss of Don Sjostrom, I need Paul. He is the right man to replace Don."

If you and the Ambassador agree to my putting Paul on my operations officer roles, Paul will resign from IVS. USAID will need to hire him as a contractor starting this minute, with your approval."

I did not even know there was pressure to move me. Sam Thong was "off-limits" to almost all Americans in Laos, including those at

headquarters in Vientiane. It was considered a "TOP SECRET" operation. All communication with and travel to Sam Thong required explicit approval by the Mission Director and Ambassador. That approval was not customarily granted, so routine communication was limited.

Sam Thong, known by its map coordinates as Lima Site 20, and a companion site across the mountain from Sam Thong, known as Lima Site 20 Alternate (Long Tieng), were the headquarters of America's support for the Hmong in northeast Laos. Sam Thong was the base for USAID's civilian humanitarian assistance to refugees, including a massive medical program. Long Tieng was the base for the CIA's field operation in support of General Vang Pao and his guerrilla army. The civilian and military operations worked in close coordination with one another.

There was minimal communication into or out of Sam Thong, so I knew nothing about the pressure to move forward area-serving IVS volunteers to safer places. I had not heard that an IVS volunteer in a forward area had been killed, but that information did not change my resolve to work with Pop in the refugee program.

Charlie Mann told Pop that I should first sever my relationship with IVS. Once done, he said he would immediately put me on the USAID roles as a personal services contractor, with the required paperwork to follow. Pop had Carol Mills radio to the IVS Education Chief, Bernie Wilder. Handing the microphone to me, Pop said, *"Paul, you know what to say. Tell Bernie that you are not relocating to Vientiane. Tell him that you resign from IVS. Don't let him talk you out of it."*

I resigned, and Bernie accepted my resignation without protest or arguments. I agreed to follow up by submitting a written resignation, which I would deliver when I next traveled to Vientiane.

Pop shook my hand and said, *"Congratulations, Paul. You just made a big move, from IVS volunteer to USAID refugee relief and rehabilitation officer."* I was amazed! In a few seconds, I went from being a Peace Corps-like volunteer to a U.S. Government contractor, and I was working in the job of my dreams, as a refugee officer for the Hmong.

There had been no discussion of salary, work scope, work hours, or vacation time. That would all come in time. The important thing was that, like magic, I was now in a position I had long desired. And things kept moving fast. That same day, Pop sent me to a refugee village to begin learning the ropes as a refugee officer, accompanied by one of his best local staff, Her Tou.

For a few months, Pop and his key staffers put me through a series of tests. I wasn't aware that I was being tested, but I was. I successfully navigated those tests. Pop's "naikongs" (Hmong leaders), village headmen, key military leaders, and local-hired USAID staff had seen other Americans fail Pop's tests and leave Sam Thong disappointed. So the staff had reserved, fully accepting me until Pop made it clear that I had passed his tests. Pop made it clear with his actions, and only then did many raise their hands in a "wei" and greet me as "one of Pop's boys."

Pop's signal came when he gave me a specific role in the refugee operation. That came several months after I had started going "to the field" as a refugee officer. One morning at the Quonset Hut, Pop gave me a mandate. *"Paul, you've done a good job. You work well with the Hmong. Everyone is pleased with you."*

Pop continued, *"We work closely with the Hmong and their leader, General Vang Pao. However, the General's Special Guerrilla Unit army is not just made up of Hmong soldiers. Other hill tribes are also aligned with the General and supported by our CIA colleagues in Long Tieng."*

"There is a hill tribe called the Lao Theung. They are said to be the original inhabitants of Laos, living in these mountains long before the Lao, Thai, and Hmong came down to Laos from China. Their leader is named Xieng Man Noi. He is one of General Vang Pao's most respected field commanders."

"We don't pay enough attention to the Lao Theung. They are among the fiercest guerrilla warriors fighting against the Pathet Lao and North Vietnamese regular army troops. The Lao Theung are called the Khmu or Kha. They are dark-skinned and speak a unique language different from the Chinese-based, highly tonal Lao or Hmong languages. Lao Theung cracks and snaps rather than being tonal. It sounds more like Malay or Indonesian."

"The legends say that when God created people, he fashioned them from clay in a fire. The Lao Theung were the last people out of the fire. That is why their skin color is so dark. And when they exited the fire, it was sputtering and spitting. That is why their language cracks and snaps."

After the history lesson, Pop said. *"With your dark skin, you are my perfect operations officer to build a close relationship of trust with the Lao Theung. I want you to focus on them. With increased Vietnamese hunger for Lao territory, General Vang Pao needs the Lao Theung more than ever, and our refugee program needs to provide better support to them."*

"I want you to spend time with Xieng Man Noi. Provide whatever refugee supplies his refugee villages need. Become his closest friend and supporter.

Make meeting their needs your priority. Paul, you will be my Khmu tribe specialist."

That same day, I flew from Sam Thong to the mountainous area between Luang Prabang and Xieng Khouang Provinces. Over the following months, I spent many nights in Lao Theung villages, sleeping in the huts of village or military leaders, eating with the people, and getting to know and supporting their refugee relief needs with rice, protein, milk, cooking pots, plastic sheeting for shelter, agricultural tools, seeds, fertilizer, and insecticide.

I also provided medicine and school supplies, helped villagers build schools and health clinics, and worked with Xieng Man Noi to identify youth to be trained by USAID and Hmong authorities as nurses, medics, and schoolteachers in Sam Thong training facilities.

Often, I would start my trips to Lao Theung villages with a visit to Xieng Man Noi. We would develop a plan, and then I would travel with him or one of his leaders to the Lao Theung villages he designated. Xieng Man Noi and I became friends as well as counterparts.

I learned a lot about the Lao Theung. The word Lao Theung means upland Lao. They were called that because they were middle-mountain dwellers. They lived in the lower heights of mountains as opposed to the Lao Loum (lowland Lao), who lived in the river valleys, or the Lao Sung (High Lao) or Hmong, who lived on the mountain tops.

Lao Theung culture was distinct from Lao or Hmong culture. The Lao Theung were animists, like the Hmong, rather than Buddhists, like the lowland Lao. Lao Theung believed in spirits of Nature that either protected them or caused them great harm and grief. Adherence to Lao Theung societal rules and norms would invoke support from the spirits. Ignoring or violating societal norms would invoke the wrath of the spirits.

Xieng Man Noi was the overall Lao Theung commander. Under him were village self-defense forces. Because local military leaders had access to outside resources, they wielded more authority than traditional civilian leaders. Rural Laos had no electricity, running water for toilets, roads, or cash economy. The day began at sunrise and ended at sunset. The only entertainment was sitting in the village leader's hut around a central fire at night, sharing a meal, drinking local brew, and conversing.

There were no hotels or restaurants in Lao Theung villages. I usually stayed in the hut of one of the paramilitary or civilian leaders. I felt like Margaret Mead or Franz Boas. I would spend hours around the fire at night conversing about Lao Theung culture. My challenge was knowing how Lao Theung culture differed from Lao Loum and Lao Sung cultures and neighboring Thai, Vietnamese, and Chinese cultures.

I used Laotian, but I was starting to understand Lao Theung. I began making a list of borrowed words from the Lao language, Thai, Chinese, and Vietnamese. Using borrowed words indicates the village's migration patterns, who villagers had been in contact with, and even possibly who they might still be influenced by.

I spent time learning about the social mores and customs of the Lao Theung people, identifying their basic human needs that could be satisfied with the U.S. refugee assistance program, and understanding what I could do to better support Xieng Man Noi and his people in this part of war-torn Laos.

One day, Xieng Man Noi and I were waiting for a helicopter to take us from his home village to a distant Lao Theung village. Xieng Man Noi asked, *"Mr. Paul, did you know that North Vietnamese and Pathet Lao communists also visit Lao Theung villages? I am not talking about soldiers. The visitors are political operatives."*

"Like you, they spend time with our people. Of course, they are very different from you. You bring rice and food for our people. Those visitors confiscate rice and food for their causes. Rather than giving us sustenance as you do, they take our chickens and pigs. They demand part of our crops. I am not talking about the villages I take you to. Those villages are solidly under my control. I am talking about the "no-man's-land" and "contested area" villages."

"The communists do not train our villagers to be medics, nurses, or teachers. They do not build health clinics and grade school classrooms like you do. Only America does that. The communists recruit our able-bodied men and women to carry their weapons and bullets down the Ho Chi Minh Trail from North Vietnam to the South. They recruit our young men into their communist army just like I recruit villagers into General Vang Pao's army."

"Mr. Paul, you support my people in many ways. You have great respect for our Lao Theung history and culture. You ask about it. You try to understand it. And I see how you then use that knowledge to better "fit" your programs to our culture and needs.

The villages you visit are very pleased with your support, and I am as well." They welcome you and treasure your presence. Those villagers do not welcome communist visitors. They feel used by the communists. They are loyal to General Vang Pao."

Hearing that made me feel pretty proud. I was especially pleased with the way Xieng Man Noi spoke about my role as a refugee operations officer. He noted that I was doing my best to understand and meet his people's needs.

But then, Xieng Man Noi dropped a bomb that shook my world. He hit me with something I had never thought about before!

Xieng Man Noi said in a hushed and careful voice, *"There is another big difference between you and the communists. It happens around the fire at night. You use that time to learn about us, to ask about our history, to learn about our relationships with others, and to better understand our language and culture. That is all good! But...., it is all rooted in the past."*

"When your communist counterparts spend the night in a Lao Theung village, they don't talk about the past. They talk about the future. They talk about a golden time that will come when the Americans, French, and other foreign devils have been driven into the South China Sea.

"They talk about a beautiful time that is coming when we Lao Theung people will own airplanes and helicopters. When we Lao Theung people will own all the rice, the cooking oil, the seeds, and fertilizer, they talk about a soon-to-come future when we Lao Theung people will oversee everything rather than relying on foreigners. We will not need to be recipients of gifts depending on foreign largesse. They talk about a golden future when Lao Theung will be in charge."

" That future-oriented talk gives young people "hope" that things will change for the better. They are told, and they believe that their lives will be better when all the foreigners are driven out of Laos. They are encouraged to work to achieve that bright and golden future."

Xieng Man Noi added, *"I know those communists are just using empty words and promises. Worthless propaganda. But it is very effective propaganda! People in the villages believe what is being said because it is said with such passion and fervor. They hang onto every word. They commit to that bright future because it is so much better than where they are now. The key word is "hope."*

"You talk about the past and give things. The communists talk about the future and give hope."

I was stunned by the direct simplicity of Xieng Man Noi's words and how different they were from my own thoughts. I had always separated what I was doing from the war effort and politics.

The IVS tradition was to be apolitical. We knew that the CIA and the military were providing guns and bullets to the Lao for the war effort. But that was not us. We knew that the CIA was training soldiers and pilots. That was not us. We were proud that we were not involved in the war. We were doing good things - giving poor people the wherewithal to survive in a difficult situation not of their choosing. We were helping people to survive by giving them basic human needs "stuff" as the war raged around them.

IVSers would say, and I often said, *"If not us, then who will do this valuable humanitarian service?"* We all knew the answer—no one. We were pleased to be humanitarian workers for peace rather than military warriors.

Xieng Man Noi had challenged that stance. His eye-opening soliloquy revealed to me in a visceral gut punch not whether the "altruistic above politics" view is right or wrong but how others view those doing humanitarian work in a war zone. I was shocked, but I also understood what he was saying.

The communists said they were helping to usher in a bright new world of local control by driving the foreign devils and their running lackey dogs out of Laos. They said that soon, all corrupt government officials, amoral military, and the foreign conspirators who prop them up would be gone. That all foreigners were part of the problem, not the solution.

"We communists are just like you villagers. Laos is our home. We are not from strange places across the sea. We were here yesterday; we are here today, and we will be here tomorrow. We will never board our airplanes and fly away to distant lands. We won't even walk away."

"We are your hope for a better future, peace, and prosperity. That will happen when Laos is freed from the evil influences of the foreign devil war-mongers and their running lackey dogs."

I had never once associated what I was doing with the Cold War -- with Russia and China versus America or communism versus democracy. I had never thought about my refugee assistance as an integral part of America's Cold War strategy. Xieng Man Noi was letting me know that my innocent and pure motives were not seen as such by all. He was saying that I was seen as a "political operative" in spite of my "do-good" attitude.

His observations woke me up! The more I thought about it, the more I realized how naive I had been and how naive many of my IVS volunteer friends were. Regardless of our personal beliefs about the war, to the recipients of our humanitarian assistance, we were part of a much bigger political machine. "Hard" and "soft" support were two sides of the same coin.

The communists had no supplies, food, or airplanes to ride in. However, they did have the gift of "hope" for a better future. Rather than meeting today's pressing refugee needs with assistance, they were successfully selling hope for a brighter future.

Xieng Man Noi was right. America's support for refugee village women and children could also be seen as support for military dependents. That support allowed husbands to fight on the battlefield, knowing their families were being cared for. When our refugee program moved refugees from harm's way to a safer resettlement area, that provided a rationale for the soldiers to cede territory and move. When support was provided to keep refugees in place, a strong rationale was provided for troops to hold territory and fight to protect their families.

Over the next few days, I pondered Xieng Man Noi's teaching. After some introspection, I decided that the humanitarian aid I provided and America's effort to contain communism were the right things to do. I had seen how savage communism was. I felt local leaders' and villagers' distaste for communism's rigid control. I saw and knew of Pathet Lao and North Vietnamese atrocities and abuses. Communism is a brutal system.

I also knew the war would continue with or without me. I believed that the humanitarian assistance provided by America would dwindle and die if civilian support for refugees were to end.

For those reasons, I decided to continue working in the program when IVS volunteers were starting to reject working in Laos with U.S. funding. They no longer wanted to be associated with the war effort, not even the humanitarian side of it.

Xieng Man Noi introduced me to a different way of thinking. While I was not in Laos for a political purpose and did not come to wage war or even support America's Cold War stance, I decided I was comfortable being seen as a political operative because I was confident that what I was doing was right.

It became clear that my job was to do what I could, the best way possible, where I was and where I wanted to be. Thanks to Xieng Man Noi.

What a teacher this unexpected mountain warrior and sage Xieng Man Noi was! His lessons have served me in many ways over the years in many circumstances. I developed a simple three-part process for applying Xieng Man Noi's teaching in my personal and professional life.

First, I view a circumstance at the micro level. What am I doing with a specific client or beneficiary group? How am I impacting their lives?

Second, I view larger pictures – including the largest possible macro level. In the case of refugee assistance, how does what I've been asked to do fit in increasingly larger circles – the politics of war in northeast Laos, Southeast Asia, and the Cold War?

At the micro- and especially the macro-level, I accept that I am mostly on the outside looking in. I will never fully understand all the reasons, ramifications, and justifications for any given policy or approach. However, my responsibility is to practice due diligence about the context and implications to the best of my ability.

Third, after thoroughly analyzing the micro- and macro-implications, I must ultimately decide what to do. The key is my comfort level. Do I feel comfortable in my heart of hearts?

The closer to the action, the more weight should be given. I am comfortable giving more weight to the micro-analysis than to macro-analysis, and my final decision must be on "my terms." I must be willing to take full responsibility for my decisions and my actions.

Over my career, I have followed that process with twists and turns. It is not a perfect approach, but it has served me well, and thanks for this valuable life lesson go to a most unexpected teacher: Lao Theung warlord Xieng Man Noi.

LOK SOK

How often had I quietly whispered, *"Paul, why are you here?"* The question is sometimes existential, sometimes only situational.

First, Let me share some background.

It was the summer of 1974. I was in my early 30's. I had just completed a six-year tour as a foreign service officer. Not in London, Paris, or Rome. My service had been in a red-hot war zone. This was during the Vietnam War, and I was working with war refugees in the misty mountains and tangled high jungles of northeast Laos, less than 150 miles from North Vietnam's capital city, Hanoi.

The geography of northeast Laos was rugged mountains. There were no roads, no electricity, or running water. People lived as they had for thousands of years, mostly as subsistence (swidden) farmers. In that war zone, being in the wrong place at the wrong time meant certain death - from the barrel of a North Vietnamese communist's AK 47 assault rifle.

Over those six years, especially in dangerous situations, but also sometimes from physical discomfort, I had asked myself on repeated occasions, *"Paul, why are you here?"*

One easy answer was that it was exhilarating in a James Bond-like way. However, I never found a satisfying answer to that persistent and vexing question.

And now, in my follow-on assignment, I was again asking myself that very same question. The State Department had transferred me from the communist-infested jungles of Laos to the U.S. Embassy in the storied capital city of Cambodia – Phnom Penh.

I had visited Cambodia several times during my vacations. I remembered Phnom Penh as an exotic, peaceful, sleepy, backwater town. Water buffaloes meandered on the city's broad boulevards. Magnificent ruins of an ancient Khmer kingdom were scattered around Phnom Penh, and the royal palace and the Buddhist temples were spectacular in size and resplendent in beauty.

I thought that my Phnom Penh assignment would be a much-needed respite from the strain and stress of living in the malarial jungles of Laos while trying to avoid communist bullets.

I had just married. My father had also recently passed away, and because I was an only child, my mother had come to live with my wife and me in Washington, DC, while I was studying Cambodian in preparation for my assignment.

In orientation, I learned that my wife and mother could not accompany me to Cambodia. It was too dangerous for dependents. They would have to live in the safety of Bangkok, Thailand, and my time would be divided. Every month, after three weeks of working 7 days a week in Cambodia, I would be allowed one week of rest and recuperation with my family in Bangkok.

That was not what I had been expecting. It got worse. When I visited Cambodia on vacation, Phnom Penh was a town of 400,000 inhabitants. But malice had descended on Cambodia. Like ISIS of today, and like the Nazis in Europe during World War II, the godless Khmer Rouge (Red Cambodians) were an evil presence in what had been a peaceful nation.

The Khmer Rouge soldiers were a ruthless cult of death, and their leader, Pol Pot, lorded over a blood-drenched reign of terror that forced villagers to flee to Phnom Penh from their rural homes to escape Khmer Rouge barbarism.

Because of the influx of refugees, Phnom Penh's population had swelled to more than 2 million people. Most lived in absolute squalor, and the city's infrastructure could not support such a large population. My job was to provide shelter, water, and food to Phnom Penh's large and, every day growing more desperate refugee population.

Much of the countryside had fallen to the Khmer Rouge communists, and even Phnom Penh was a city under siege. The Khmer Rouge had interdicted all major roadways into the city, and the vital Mekong River artery was closed due to Khmer Rouge attacks on boats trying to bring food and supplies into the city.

Khmer Rouge soldiers were gobbling up the remaining Royal Government-controlled land in the countryside. They would attack Government soldiers who were protecting a town or village. The Government soldiers sometimes abandoned their posts.

When they fought, they were almost always routed by Pol Pot's ruthless killing machine.

Once the Khmer Rouge were in control of a village or town, they would identify all government officials – nurses, medics, teachers, politicians, and soldiers. The officials would be forced to dig a mass grave. The officials would then be lined up in front of their grave site, shot in the back of the head, or beheaded with knives to save ammunition.

Their dead bodies would be kicked into the mass grave. After that mass murder, villagers would be submissive. If they could escape, they would flee to Phnom Penh.

With Phnom Penh under siege and the refugee population burgeoning, rice, cooking oil, protein, milk, cooking pots, and plastic sheeting for temporary shelter had to be airlifted into Phnom Penh from Thailand. The Embassy Refugee Office ran an airlift operation like the Berlin airlift of World War II. It was a 24/7 responsibility. Refugee officers worked 15 hours a day, 7 days a week. It was exhausting work and extremely dangerous.

In the late fall of 1974, after the monsoon season was over, the Khmer Rouge communists began a final military assault to topple the monarchy and seize power in Phnom Penh. Under cover of night, Khmer Rouge soldiers would position Russian- and Chinese-made "Katusha" rockets in the no man's land surrounding Phnom Penh. Dozens of rockets were launched into the city every night.

The 'Katusha" rockets carried powerful explosive warheads, but the rockets had no guidance system. The Khmer Rouge soldiers would point the rockets in a general direction and launch them. Without control, the rockets would fall willy-nilly where they may, making for an unnerving "wheel of fortune" randomness to the destructive power of the enemy's rockets.

In Laos, to be safe, you simply had to avoid being in a place where the North Vietnamese or communist Pathet Lao soldiers were. It was not that simple in Cambodia. No matter where you might be, you were a random target when rockets rained into the city. You could run but could not hide.

You would first hear a dull "pop" at night as a rocket was launched. Next, overhead, you would hear a *"shrill whistle"* (much like a 4th of July rocket sound). Then, if you were lucky, and luck had everything to do with it, you would hear the *"boom"* of a distant explosion. If you did not hear an explosion, the rocket was a "dud," or you had taken a direct hit. A direct hit meant certain death - from the rocket or its shrapnel.

Life in that environment was more difficult than I had experienced or imagined. Hunger, disease, and pestilence were everywhere in the refugee camps. We refugee officers worked from the break of dawn until late at night or until we dropped from exhaustion. We were too few, and the resources we controlled were not sufficient to meet the ever-increasing needs.

I asked myself several times a day, especially at night when the killer rockets whistled relentlessly in the dark sky, *"Paul, what did you get yourself into? Why are you here?"*

I felt I was doing a lot of good by assisting people in desperate need. But was the sacrifice worth it? I thought so, but I was not sure.

In early December 1974, I was summoned to the Ambassador's

office. Ambassador John Gunther Dean was a recently arrived Ambassador. I had a severe issue with the Ambassador shortly after his arrival. He had shouted at me and questioned my judgment about a topic I knew well. After that, I avoided Ambassador Dean. Now, I was being summoned to his office.

Ambassador Dean was a very dapper and fancy man. With his carefully combed, peppery black-grey hair and in a diplomatic grey pin-striped suit, he looked out of place in Cambodia's chaotic work environment.

96

Ambassador Dean was a man of supreme confidence. He would never ask himself, *"Who am I?"* Or *"Why am I here?"*

On that day, Ambassador Dean was all smiles. *"Sit down, Paul!"* He gestured to me to sit in a chair in front of his massive desk. A fluent French speaker, the Ambassador was German-born and had a slightly European accent. Ambassador Dean continued, *"Paul, I heard you are quite a magician. Cambodia's Prime Minister requested that the U.S. Embassy put on a Christmas show for a large Cambodian orphanage. I want you, Paul, to organize our Embassy's response. And I want you to perform a magic show at the orphanage!"*

Every fiber in my body wanted to say, *"No!"* But I saw no escape from Ambassador Dean's direct order. I reluctantly agreed, with a condition. *"My wife is my magic assistant. You must lift your ban on dependent travel and permit my wife to come to Phnom Penh with my mother. My mother cannot be left in Bangkok alone. And I need my magic equipment. It is in Bangkok."*

Ambassador Dean agreed that my wife and mother could come to Phnom Penh and leave the day after the show. The "milk run" would transport them. On the appointed day, December 20, 1974, my wife and mother flew in from Bangkok on the Embassy courier flight. My magic equipment was with them.

We had several hours before the show, so I took my wife and mother to see one of my refugee camps. We drove some 5 kilometers out of the city. I noticed that on the road to the refugee camp, women who, on most days, sold coconuts and mangos were not hawking on the side of the road. Something was wrong. I parked the jeep on the main road and asked my wife and mother to stay in it. I got out and walked down a narrow path to the refugee camp and village—a several-minute walk.

Nobody was on the trail. When I reached the entrance to the camp, I saw a horrific sight. Impaled on a bamboo stake was the bloody severed head of a 5- or 6-year-old girl. I knew that was the brutal handiwork of the Khmer Rouge.

Later, I learned that there had been a firefight the previous night. Villagers and refugees abandoned their homes and tents. They hid in the forest as Government soldiers retreated. The victorious Khmer Rouge soldiers entered the village to loot and plunder.

Not everyone heard the sounds of fighting. The small girl who had been beheaded was deaf. She did not hear the firefight and, in the rush to escape, the family missed waking her. The Khmer Rouge soldiers beheaded her and made her a symbol of their death cult.

They intended to instill fear in the villagers and refugees. It certainly worked to instill fear in me.

When I saw the lifeless, bloody head, my body recoiled. I uttered a choked scream, my legs gave away, and I fell backward. My body repelled away from the horrifying sight, and now, on the ground, I could not take my eyes off the lifeless, bloody head.

My thoughts turned to my wife and mother, who were alone in the jeep on the main road. I struggled to my feet. On weak legs, I ran as fast as I could. As I ran, I asked myself, *"Paul, why are you here?"*

At the jeep, my wife saw my expression. Sweat was pouring from my forehead. I was trembling. Color had drained from my face. *"Paul, are you OK? Are you going to take us to the refugee camp?"*

This was a time to be oblique. *"It is not a good time to visit the refugee camp. We need to set up the magic show. Let's go now!*

When we reached the orphanage, I was still shaking. I focused on the set-up. My wife, mother, and I quickly arranged the stage for the magic show and soon, several hundred Cambodian orphans crowded into the small auditorium. It had once been a French movie theater, but now, in total disrepair, the kids sat on a dirt floor in front of an old, dilapidated stage. Nuns and other adults stood behind the rows of sitting children.

My first act was the Benares Temple. It was an ornate box painted to look like a Hindu temple. The temple's front doors were open in the center of the stage, with a dozen swords piercing it. It appeared empty. All that could be seen inside the temple was the glitter of the crisscrossed sword blades in the darkness of an otherwise empty chamber.

The audience was hushed, not knowing what to expect. Recorded Hindu music began to play, and my wife slowly walked to center stage from behind the stage right curtain.

Dressed in a traditional Indian sari, the audience gasped. Those kids probably had never seen a live stage show before. My wife smiled and greeted the audience with the traditional "Wei" (two hands clasped together in front of the body). As the audience leaned forward to watch, my wife gracefully removed the twelve swords. Once removed, she gestured to show the audience that the temple was empty.

Closing the two front doors, my wife stepped away. As she did, two flames flashed before the temple, emitting thick, white smoke. The audience gasped again. As the smoke disappeared, they saw a resplendently dressed Hindu man wearing a royal purple robe and a deep red turban sitting in what had been an empty temple. That Hindu man was me!

I stood, greeted the audience, and walked to the front of the stage.

"Chimreap sua, Lok e Lok Sray!" (Good afternoon, ladies and gentlemen.)

My American-accented Cambodian was understandable. The kids greeted me with a Wei and then with shouts and applause. Excited by my very magical and unexpected appearance, the applause was loud and long.

Things were going well—until they were not!

As the applause died down, I began my opening patter and magic. Then - *"sniff, sniff, sniff"* – I smelled something burning. Glancing to stage right, I saw my wife in a panic. Sparks from the flashes of fire had set the very dusty, dry stage curtain on fire. The bottom of the curtain was in open flames.

I knew I had to quell the fire quickly. I sprang into action. Fortunately, a large bucket of water was on stage for use later in the magic show. I threw water on the burning curtain, stomped on the flames with my feet, and even pressed my hands down onto the smoldering cloth to extinguish the last flames.

Somehow, I managed to put the fire out, but in doing so, I must have wiped the sweat from my face with my sooty hands. That deposited black soot all over my sweaty face, making me look like

a young Al Jolson in vaudeville blackface. Of course, when your face is black, you don't need to put on blackface. I looked silly.

My wife rescued me. She carefully wiped the soot from my face as I stood out of view on one side of the stage. Looking better but still quaking from the accidental fire, I returned to center stage to continue with the magic show. I was embarrassed and asked myself, *"Paul, why are you here?"*

"Kids," I said in Cambodian, *"I need a volunteer. If you want to help the magician, please raise your hand."* Dozens of hands went up. I scanned the audience. There were many bright-eyed kids to choose from, but my eyes stuck on one small boy in the second row.

I walked down from the stage and out into the audience. Kids were screaming and fidgeting with excitement. I took the hand of the small boy I had focused on. Pulling him to his feet, I guided him up onto the stage.

When the audience saw who I had selected, they made a sucking air sound like Asians do when they are puzzled or perplexed.

Moments later, I understood why.

I smiled at the small boy and asked him in Cambodian, *"Chumuuh eh- lok?"* (What is your name?) The boy didn't respond. He just looked at me with wide eyes.

I could tell that the audience was nervous. *"Kyom niyea Khmae, lok."* (Young boy, I am speaking Cambodian to you.) I asked his name again. He didn't respond. He just stood there looking at me with wide eyes.

I had been drawn to this small boy. I didn't know why, but now I understood why the audience reacted to my selection.

Perhaps I had selected a boy who was mentally challenged or a deaf-mute.

I wanted this number to be a showstopper, especially after the disastrous fire. I was facing a double disaster! I again asked myself, *"Paul, what are you doing here?"*

The show must go on, so I continued with the small boy. Escorting him back to the audience and selecting someone else would be embarrassing for the boy and a "downer" for the show. I had to improvise. I did.

Smiling, I showed the boy an empty box. I waved my magic wand. A live rabbit appeared in the box! The boy visibly reacted with a surprised look. I held the rabbit close to the boy and said in Cambodian, *"Lok – lok,"* (Little boy), *"Chaat ni chomuuh Peter."* (This rabbit is named Peter.) *"Peter wants to know your name."*

He did not respond, but he had an excited smile on his face, so I continued. I signaled for him to watch me. I placed the rabbit in another box, gave the boy the magic wand, and gestured for him to wave it in the air. As he waved the wand, the rabbit vanished from the box!

The little boy ran to the box. He looked inside with a baffled expression on his face. Then, he turned to me and asked excitedly, *"Chaat thu naa?"* (Where did the rabbit go?)

The audience gasped and then broke into thunderous applause. In my years of magic, I had never heard applause that loud, and it continued getting louder and louder. The applause did not stop. Kids were shouting and cheering. So were the adults.

I had no idea why the audience was so excited.

Baffled by the rabbit's disappearance, the boy was still looking for Peter. Finally, the audience settled down, wanting to know what was next. When their attention was back on stage, I made Peter reappear with a wave of the magic wand.

I held Peter so the small boy could pet him. Looking at Peter, the small boy smiled, looked at me, and then said directly to Peter, **"*Kynom huh, Sok.*"** (My name is SOK.)

I was relieved. The boy had finally said his name. I was not prepared for what happened after he spoke. Kids and adults began shouting and cheering again, but louder than before. Everyone in the audience was celebrating, and the uproar wasn't subsiding.

I took Sok off the stage and led him back to where he had been sitting. The nuns all ran to him, hugging him and congratulating him with tears in their eyes. Kids came to talk to Sok. They clasped their hands together in front of their bodies in a "wei" to congratulate Sok.

The magic show was forgotten for a long time, but after more than 30 minutes, there was a lull. I quickly did a closing magic trick and ended the magic show. I had never seen that kind of audience reaction. I realized the applause was for my assistant, Sok, and not me. But why?

The head nun came onto the stage. She thanked me for the performance and motioned for me to walk with her to her office. A thin whisp of a woman in a wrinkled and worn habit, the old nun was as wrinkled as was her habit. Although wrinkled, her face beamed with an expression of total excitement.

The old nun reached out and gently touched my arm. Looking at me with almost colorless eyes, she said in Cambodian, *"It was a miracle!"* Then she told me Sok's story.

Sok's parents had been village officials – a teacher and a nurse. A Khmer Rouge attack on their village ended with the ruthless soldiers killing all village officials, including Sok's parents. The Khmer Rouge soldiers beheaded his mother and father. Their lifeless bodies were kicked into a mass grave while a terrified Sok watched.

That atrocity had happened three years prior. From that traumatic night forward, Sok had never spoken to anyone. After a year of not talking, his village sent Sok to the orphanage. Sok still had not uttered one word at the orphanage over the two years he had been there. Everyone at the orphanage loved him, but no one had heard Sok speak or make a vocal sound.

Yet, on that magic show afternoon, December 20, 1974, Sok encountered a rabbit named Peter. When Sok spoke to the rabbit, the spell that had silenced him was broken. After three years of silence, Sok's talking explained the overjoyed audience's reaction.

Real magic took place that afternoon when Sok's self-imposed silence ended thanks to a rabbit named Peter.

The old nun looked at me, smiled a toothless smile and warmly said, *"Magician...., it was a miracle!"*

I felt that moment in the deepest part of me! A dazzling clarity descended that gave me goosebumps. My arm hair stood on end. I felt electrified. Where there previously were questions, confusion, and chaos, there now was coherence. I now knew the answer to the question I had asked myself many times - *"Paul, why are you here?"*

Everything I had ever done in my life had prepared me for that moment on that stage with a boy named Sok and a rabbit named Peter. I had been guided to learn magic, travel to Asia, be assigned to Cambodia, and be at that orphanage on that day and on that stage. I was guided to select that one voiceless boy from the many children with raised hands.

I no longer had to ask, *"Why?"* The answer was clear. *"Things could not have been otherwise."* Everything in my life had inextricably led me to that one magical moment - to that miracle!

The nun had quietly left me alone, giving me much-needed solitude. I sat in her office until the powerful emotion subsided enough for me to stand and walk to where my wife and mother were waiting. I told them the *"rest of the story."*

Sometimes, the most profound questions are answered in the most mysterious ways. When the time was right, I was prepared! I was called! I heard the call! I was mindful! And a miracle happened!

Our God works in mysterious ways.

Magic with Cambodian royalty and refugee kids, circa 1974

Magic in Cambodia with mother and wife

Cambodia, floating Somphon on a flying carpet

Paul in turban producing a dove, circa 1974

A BOY NAMED SUE

This vignette combines my childhood life in Brazil, Indiana, with my Cold War experience.

A country song by Johnny Cash - *A Boy Named Sue* – forever changed my life. *A Boy Named Sue* is about a boy whose father gave him a girl's name. The boy goes on a quest to find his father and exact revenge on him from the barrel of a gun. The first couple of verses go something like this:

"My daddy left home when I was about three. He didn't leave much for my maw and me, just this old guitar and an empty bottle of booze. I don't blame him cause he run and hid, but the meanest thing that old man ever did, before he left, he went and named me Sue.

He must have thought it was a pretty good joke, and it got a lot of laughs from a lot of folks, but it seems I had to fight and struggle my whole life through.

Some gal would giggle, and I'd get red, some guy would laugh, and I'd have to bust his head. Life ain't easy when you're a boy named Sue."

Why was that country song an epiphany for me? Just think about it. If your skin color was as dark as mine is and your last name was WHITE, you too would understand the CRUEL irony of growing up being a Boy named Sue. This story might not be pretty or feel just right, but when you've read it, I hope you will understand what it was like, growing up as a Boy Named Sue or a BLACK named WHITE.

Let's start in 1947 – my first day in primary school. The teacher seated us in alphabetical order. I was sitting in the very last chair of the very last row.

From the back of the room, I watched my classmates stand, say their names, acknowledge the applause, and then sit down. Finally, it was my turn - my first public speech, my Icebreaker.

I stood and said, *"My name is Paul – Paul WHITE."* I waited for the applause. There was none. I saw a ripple of surprise as I looked at that sea of white faces. Then, I heard an explosion of laughter. The class was laughing at my color and my name. My classmates were laughing at me! Even the teacher laughed.

The pain of the sound of that laughter was forever etched on my heart and burned in my memory.

With time, I could share hundreds of name-calling incidents and ugly-word stories from my childhood. But that one story is enough to give you a flavor of what it was like growing up a person of color in the 'good old days of yesteryear.' Fast-forward to 1954. I was entering junior high school. As a boy, I recited daily the old saw, *"Sticks and stones may break my bones, but your words will never hurt me."*

That was a big lie. Their words did hurt. Now, as a teenager, I wanted to say something more powerful – that would hurt the perpetrator as much as he or she wanted to hurt me. I asked my father, *"How do you handle racial slurs about your color and your name?"*

My father was silent for a long time. He took a draw on his cigarette, exhaled a cloud of smoke, and said, *"Son, never use anger. Take the high road. Seek a humorous way out or a diversion. If you can't find humor or diversion, don't say anything. Look the person in the eye, smile, then turn and walk away. Leave them in a befuddled cloud of confusion."*

I did not respond, but I thought to myself, *"Wow! That is the dumbest advice I have ever heard."* Those words drove an even larger wedge between me and my father. When I graduated from high school in 1959, my goal was to go as far away from southern Indiana as possible and as far from my father as possible. I went to college in California, graduate school in Hawaii, became a graduate exchange student in Japan, and then started my career as a foreign service officer in Laos—half a world away from Indiana and my father.

Fast forward to 1970. After years of working and living in the high jungle of northeast Laos, I was assigned to Luang Prabang, Laos' royal capital. My assigned house was a beautiful French chalet. It had running water, electricity, and even a full kitchen.

What a change from sleeping in bamboo and thatch huts in jungle villages. I didn't own any cooking utensils and didn't know how to cook, so I began to frequent a Chinese restaurant near my house. The food was delicious and inexpensive.

The owners were three brothers, recent immigrants from China. Their names were Sing, Seng, and Song. They spoke limited English and did not speak any Lao. After I had eaten in their restaurant for several days, the brothers suggested that I pay monthly rather than on a meal-by-meal basis—*"Good for you, good for we."* I agreed.

Often, I was the only customer in their tiny restaurant. When I walked in, I would hear, *"Mr. White, how you today? Mr. White, what did you eat today? Mr. White, good taste food today?"*

After the first month, Sing gave me the bill. It was a work of art— meticulously handwritten on a big sheet of newsprint. It was mainly in Chinese, but I could read the numbers. The total for the month was 20,000 kip for the 70 or 80 meals I had eaten that month. (20,000 kip was the equivalent of $30.) Everything in Laos was inexpensive, especially if you were paid in U.S. dollars.

But there was something wrong with the bill. I hesitated, causing great concern. *"Mr. White, you have problem? Too much kip?"*

The problem was not the amount of the bill. I had studied Japanese. Japanese and Chinese are written with similar characters. While I could not speak Chinese, I could read some characters. That allowed me to catch the brothers playing what they thought would be an inside joke. At the top of that work-of-art bill, in large red Chinese characters, the brothers had written the character for BLACK rather than WHITE.

The bill was titled, "MONTHLY BILL FOR Mr. BLACK!"

I said confusedly, *"Sing, Seng, and Song – I don't have a problem with the amount. It is fine. But this is Mr. Black's bill. I am Mr. White!"*

The three brothers stared at me in disbelief. They stared at the offending Chinese character. Then they stared at each other. "AI-

YA!" they screamed in unison before scurrying to the privacy of their tiny kitchen. For 15 minutes, I heard the loudest arguing I had ever heard.

Kitchen pots and pans clanged.

Then things went silent. Sing, Seng, and Song shuffled out of the kitchen and lined up in front of me. As Asians do when they are embarrassed, they bowed deeply. Sing said, *"Mr. White so solly! We look everywhere. No find bill Mr. White. This month, Mr. White no pay any money."*

These brothers were dirt poor. Losing one month's payment from one of their only customers might be a death blow for their business. I was extremely angry with the three brothers. The joke they had tried to play on me was reminiscent of the ugly name-calling from my childhood—something I had left home to escape.

But something happened. I did not plan what I said next. It just came out of my mouth. I laughed, breaking the tension in the room. Then I said, *"Mr. Black works at the U.S. Embassy. He is a colleague of mine. I am sorry, Mr. Black has returned to America unexpectedly this morning - a family emergency. Mr. Black asked me to pay his restaurant bill. Before leaving, he gave me the money to do so."*

Surprised at the turn of events, Sing accepted the money. The three brothers looked confused, and then they began to bow and offer me dessert graciously. On my part, I realized what had happened. My father's advice from all those years ago flooded my consciousness. *"Don't use anger, Paul. Find the humor or diversion. Take a high road!"*

That is precisely what I had done. Following my father's advice, had three very clear outcomes. First, it saved face for Sing, Seng, and Song. In Asia, saving face is a big deal!

Second, following my father's advice made a very awkward situation much better in a nanosecond. The brothers knew they had wronged and hurt me. They were so repentant, they offered to forego a month's income as an apology.

110

I was offended but also needed Sing, Seng, and Song. I realized that anger would not have resolved anything. Using humor and diversion did as my father had advised me decades earlier, was the best option for all involved.

I thought, *"How wise was my father! And how foolish was I to have laughed at and disrespected him."*

Third, through my generous action, I guaranteed myself the best food and service available in Luang Prabang for as long as I stayed in the royal capital of Laos.

Almost serendipitously, on that same day, I heard A Boy Named Sue for the first time. A friend had purchased a new Johnny Cash album from the U.S. He was playing "A Boy Named Sue" in his office as I walked by. I went in to listen to the song.

As I listened to *"A Boy Named Sue,"* the last few verses rocked my world. The boy named Sue had spent his young life searching for his dad with the intent to kill him. He finally found the old man in a dark back room of a honkytonk bar on the wrong side of the tracks.

The boy named Sue looked at his dad and shouted, *"My name is Sue. How do you do? Now you are going to die."*

The boy and his father began to brawl. When they rolled out of the bar onto the smelly muddy street, the boy named Sue drew his revolver. The bar's flashing lights made the gun barrel glisten.

The boy's father stood, wiped a trickle of blood from his lip, and said to his son: *"Son, this old world is mighty rough, and if you're gonna make it through, you gotta be tough, and I knew I wouldn't be there to help you along. So I gave you that name, and I said goodbye. I knew you'd have to get tough or die. It's that name I gave you that's made you so goldarn strong."*

"Now you just fought one hell of a fight, and I know that you hate me, and you've got the right to kill me. I wouldn't blame you if you do. But you'd better thank me before I die 'cause I put the gravel

in your gut and the spit in your eye. I'm the dirty SOB that named you Sue."

For the first time in his life, the boy understood why he was named Sue. He staggered back a step or two and said, *"I got all choked up, and I threw down my gun, and I called him my Paw, and he called me his son. And I left that honkytonk with a different point of view."*

"I think of my old paw every now and then - every time I fight and every time I win. And if I ever have a son, I'm gonna name him Mike, or John, or George - anything but Sue."

I was astounded. My life had paralleled that of the Boy Named Sue. It was as if Shel Silverstein had written the song for me. I thought about all of those wasted years when I hated my father because of the name White he had bequeathed to me - a name that had caused me so much suffering and pain. I thought about my youthful ignorance and how wrong I had been about my father's sage advice.

I knew exactly what I needed to do. I took the next available flight from Laos. Back in Indiana, I learned that my father was in the intensive care ward of the Clay County Hospital, suffering from black lung disease and emphysema.

I rushed to the hospital. My father was in a dark room under an old-fashioned oxygen tent. When I walked into the room, my father saw and recognized me even though it was dark. He tried to sit up but couldn't. He tried to speak to me, but I could not understand him because of his coughing and wheezing.

I sat on his bed, took my father's hand, and gently said, *"Shhhh, don't try to talk. I just came to tell you that you are the best father I could ever have hoped to have."*

My father did not speak for a long time. Tears welled up in his eyes. Then he squeezed my hand and smiled so brightly, it drove the darkness from that hospital room. What a defining moment for both of us. Heavy burdens were lifted from my heart - and from my father's heart as well.

If you have something you need to say to someone, don't wait. Don't hesitate. Say what you need to say now. Tomorrow is never promised!

I left Clay County Hospital with a different point of view. On that emotional night, I knew that I had set things right. What had been a dark world became clear and bright.

My attitude changed. I now hold my head high when I think of my father. I am proud of the name he gave me, Paul Edward WHITE. Thank you, Johnny Cash, for the country song you sang that reconciled me and my father, William Clarence WHITE!

W.C. White, in the backyard of 754 N. Columbia, circa 1964

Paul with mother and father in Idlewild, Michigan, circa 1964

KATUSHA

I was a Cold War Warrior, seeing and doing things that will never be talked about. In this vignette, I talk about my encounter with the Russian military and the lessons I learned.

I staggered. I stumbled. I careened from one wall to the other down a long, dark, narrow passageway.

"I know what you are thinking. No, I was not drunk. I was struggling to maintain my balance on a dilapidated Russian freighter that was pitching and yawing through the dark, turbulent, angry waters of the Hokkaido Straits somewhere between Japan and Siberia."

Before that Russian freighter, my only boat experience had been in a two-person rowboat on the Big Walnut Creek near my home in Brazil, Indiana. The BIG Walnut Creek was only ten feet wide and four feet deep. I was a landlubber with no sea legs. That is why I was struggling to keep my body from going down and my food from coming up.

The year was 1969. Communist Russia's Travel Agency, INTOURIST, had booked me on a Russian military freighter for the first leg of an incredible journey from Yokohama, Japan, to Siberia and beyond across the vast expanse of the USSR.

I had been a volunteer in Laos. Now, I was going home to Indiana in the cheapest way possible. That was from Japan to Siberia and then overland via the trans-Siberian railroad to Moscow, Leningrad, and Helsinki. From there, I would take a Pan American Airlines flight to my home in Indiana.

The beginning of that journey was not going very well. Russian sailors on the military freighter seemed to have been given orders, *"Don't fraternize with that Black, cowboy-boot-wearing Americanski."* Though far from the truth, those Russian sailors had been told that I was a CIA agent.

On that night, in that dark corridor, I was looking for the ship's bar. I might make a friend or two over a few stiff Stolichnaya

117

vodkas. I saw the door I had been looking for. I cracked it slightly to ensure I was in the right place. I was. The stench of Lattakia tobacco, stale vodka, and human sweat almost bowled me over. I heard loud boasting coming from the bar as drunk Russian sailors bragged about their conquests in the girlie bars of Yokohama, their last port of call.

I thought, *"Sailors are the same the world over."*

Forcing my way through the heavy smoke and darkness of that smelly bar, I sat at the one vacant table. The bar was jam-packed with beefy, brawny, burly, smelly Russian sailors. They reacted to my presence like bashful schoolgirls at their first junior high school dance. When I made eye contact, a sailor would avert his gaze.

When I looked away, I could feel his brazen stare burning the nape of my neck.

The Russian sailors were curious about me. *"Who is this STRANGE black Americanski? What is he doing on our freighter?"* 1969 was the height of the Cold War. Russians had been taught to hate Americans. Americans had been taught to hate Russians.

That is why the mood in that bar went from euphoric to sullen, hostile, angry silence the second I walked in.

I felt the hate. I felt out of place. I was out of place. I was an American interloper in the lair of the enemy. I asked myself, *"Paul, what are you doing on a communist freighter in the middle of the cold, dark, dangerous Hokkaido Straits?"*

For far too long, I sat unattended. Then, a sailor approached my table. His scowl showed his contempt for me. So did his actions. He slammed a dirty, chipped tumbler on the table, poured murky, evil-smelling vodka into it, and without uttering a single word, he turned and walked away.

Bravely, I raised that tumbler in a quiet toast to the sailors sitting near me. Heads jerked away. Not even one sailor accepted my proffered friendship.

In the silent darkness of that unfriendly place, I thought, *"This was a bad idea. Maybe I should stand up and leave?"*

But my eyes had adjusted to the darkness. I saw a spinet piano in the far corner of that tiny bar. Without thinking, I stood, downed the vodka for courage, grimaced as it seared its way down my gullet, and then I made my way through the smoke and darkness to the piano.

Pressing a D minor chord, I winced at how far out of tune the piano was, but I started to play. Then, I began to sing in Russian. *"Ras vet alle, yablo y ni grushi, poplili tumani na rekoi. Vuy kodili na beryek Katusha, na vuy saki berek na krutoy."*

Because of how the piano was angled, I could only see a few sailors. Their surprised eyes were as wide as saucers as I sang that famous Russian military song, Katusha, about love and the Russian military protecting the beloved Russian motherland.

Soon, those sailors near me were singing with me. By the middle of the second verse, the room was singing with me. By the song's end, the entire room was crowded around the piano in full celebratory mode.

I played another Russian song and then another. Vodka flowed freely. The sailors sang louder and louder, and as word got out, more and more sailors crowded into the bar. Suddenly, things went silent, and sailors scrunched together, forming a narrow pathway from the door to the piano. The bar's heavy grey metal door screeched open. Sailors snapped to attention and saluted.

The captain of the ship walked into the bar.

119

The sailors wore ragged, tattered, grease-stained tee shirts and dirty, ill-fitting bell-bottomed trousers. In stark contrast, the captain was dressed in a pristine white uniform that was immaculately pressed. The uniform was decorated with heavy gold braiding and a plethora of colorful ribbons, and at the center of attention was a large red communist star.

The captain's face was chiseled. His beard was sculpted. Everything about the officer screamed, *"Patrician – Aristocrat."* I thought, *"How is that possible? I thought Russia was a class-free communist society."*

It was too crowded to stand, so I sat uncomfortably at the piano. The captain towered over me. This was the captain who, for my two days on his ship, had never welcomed me on board, had never spoken a word to me, had not even let me see him - even from a distance.

Now, we were in a classic face-to-face confrontation – two Cold War adversaries. One represented democracy, apple pie, baseball, and freedom. The other represented a godless communist nation intent on world domination.

My heart was pounding. I was on the captain's ship, surrounded by his sailors. This was a desperate situation, but I realized I had three things going for me: my natural tan, beautiful pointed-toe cowboy boots, and more handsome-than-Hollywood star-good looks. However, none of those things were working for me right then.

I asked myself, *"Paul, what would James Bond do?"*

That wasn't working either, so I focused on something more practical. I tried to hide my fear by keeping my face as inscrutable as the captain's face. We had a long, silent stare-fest.

The captain suddenly did an about-face. He barked a command to his men. I didn't understand it, but I saw the reaction. Sailors were running around every which way, as we would say in Brazil, Indiana: *"They was running like chickens with they heads cut off."*

I began a silent prayer - *"Our Father who art in heaven..."* The captain stepped back, making room for me to stand. I did, on very shaky legs. Unexpectedly, a burly Russian sailor materialized before us as I tried to gain my balance.

Surprised, my first thought was, *"Is this sailor the executioner?"* Then, I noticed that he was carrying a beautiful silver tray. On it was an exquisite decanter and two crystal vodka glasses. The sailor poured sparkling-clear vodka into the glasses. The captain took one. He motioned for me to take the other. I did.

I had another morose thought. *"Will this be my last ever drink? Am I about to become fish food in the Straits of Hokkaido? Will my parents ever know what happened to me?"*

The Russian captain raised his glass of vodka on high, looked at all the sailors, and then looked directly at me. He said, "Na za trove*!"* (To your health!) The entire room, feeling the release of tension, responded with the same toast. The sound was like a Red Navy chorus. It was the most beautiful sound I had ever heard.

With complete relief, I lifted my glass to the sailors and the captain. I returned the toast, *"Na za zdrovuie!"*

Having done what he came to do, and without another word, the captain turned and, with an expressionless face, left the bar. Soon, I was playing the piano again, and Russian sailors were singing.

Vodka was flowing freely. We celebrated for many more hours.

That summer night in 1969, at the height of the Cold War, on a Russian freighter in the Straits of Hokkaido, was a night never to be forgotten. You might be wondering why a southern Indiana yokel like me knew how to play and sing Russian songs or why I was on board that Russian military freighter during the Cold War? Was I a CIA agent? My "Clintonian" response to those questions is, "Because I could."

This very true story happened more than 50 years ago, in the foolish days of my youth. It taught me the absolute veracity of an adage. It is not the one about music taming the savage beasts. It is much simpler - MUSIC is MAGIC.

On that night, my music was the magic that enabled everyone on that Russian freighter, even the captain, to transcend the heavy weight of Cold War politics. Music made us realize an eternal truth—despite our many differences, we are all children of the same God.

In today's upside-down world where black is white and white is black, where right is wrong and wrong is right, perhaps the world would be a better place if we had far more musicians and far fewer politicians. What a peaceful world that would be!

It is said that love comes naturally. Hate must be taught. During the Cold War, we were taught to hate. Muhammed Ali had some well-chosen words about love and hate. He said with simple clarity-
"Hating people because of their color (or their politics) is wrong. And it doesn't matter what color (or political group) is doing the hating. Hating is just plain wrong!"

Those were the exact words my parents repeatedly told me as a child. I have learned that my parents were right.

PRESIDENTS I SERVED DURING THE COLD WAR AND BEYOND AND OTHER WORLD LEADERS

James Earl Carter Jr., 39th President of the United States of America

In 1976, Jimmy Carter led the Panama Canal Zone negotiations with General Omar Torrijos leading for Panama. At USAID/Panama, as Chief of the Education Office, I was responsible for overseeing the education facilities that reverted to Panama – Canal Zone College, high school, middle school, elementary school, the Canal Zone library, etc.

In the 1990s, I also worked with former President Carter in Japan, helping him to secure Japanese funding for his health projects in Africa (Guinea Worm eradication, malaria control, sanitation, and clean water projects).

Ronald Wilson Reagan, 40th President of the United States of America

President Reagan convened a National Bipartisan Commission on Central America in 1984, headed by Secretary of State Henry Kissinger. The commission's goal was to respond to a growing Russian presence and influence in Central America. I was responsible for implementing the education and training recommendations of the Kissinger Commission report. I designed one of the largest-ever USAID training program (Central America Peace Scholarships— CAPS). Basic education, curriculum strengthening, teacher training, and college textbook initiatives were also funded.

At President Reagan's request, I designed a special training initiative for students from Grenada whose studies in Cuba were truncated because of the U.S. Rescue Mission. The initiative enabled Grenadian students to enroll in American Historically Black Colleges and Universities (HBCUs). Unlike many major universities, the HBCUs recognized and allowed transfer of Cuban university credits so Grenadian could begin their study in America as Sophomores or Juniors.

George H.W. Bush, 41st President of the United States of America

1989 – With the fall of the Berlin Wall and the disintegration of the Soviet Union, doors were opened to new relationships. President George H.W. Bush and Secretary of State Baker requested USAID to assign a senior development assistance official to the U.S. Embassy in Tokyo to build a stronger U.S. – Japan economic cooperation relationship worldwide on Global Issues. I was assigned to Tokyo.

Amidst highly visible trade friction between the two countries, a new cooperation program called the U.S.-Japan Global Partnership Initiative was announced that gave priority to working with Japan in new cooperation areas for Japan. Grant funding, environment and biodiversity projects, human rights and Women in Development, HIV/AIDS and family planning, women in development, NGO partnerships, and policy projects were supported. Donor cooperation by Japan, the largest foreign aid donor, and the U.S., the second largest donor, was done to leverage the "peace dividend" stemming from the collapse of the U.S.S.R. The belief was that the two economic superpowers could accomplish much more working together than they could as foreign aid assistance competitors.

125

William Jefferson Clinton, 42nd President of the United States of America

In 1993, William Jefferson Clinton became President, representing a shift from Republican to Democrat governance. The U.S. – Japan Global Partnership was working well, so the Clinton Administration continued supporting a U.S.–Japan development assistance alliance. My Tokyo assignment was extended.

The alliance was given a new name, and minor changes in focus were made. In July 1993, the alliance was renamed - the U.S. – Japan Common Agenda for Cooperation in Global Perspective, under the leadership of Secretary of State for Global Affairs Timothy Wirth. In Tokyo, USAID expanded its work with the Ministry of Foreign Affairs, JICA, and OECF on donor cooperation issues, including biodiversity, HIV, maternal/child health, human rights, education, training, disaster assistance, women in development, and NGO collaboration programs.

An annual high-level policy coordination forum between USAID and the Ministry of Foreign Affairs was continued and expanded. The joint U.S.-Japan projects in Asia and the Pacific, Africa, Latin America, and Eastern Europe were larger than previously funded under the Global Partnership. Many U.S. Agencies participated under the overall coordination of the Under Secretary for Global Affairs.

126

George Walker Bush, 43rd President of the United States of America

President George W. Bush continued the U.S.–Japan alliance cooperation. But I was now assigned to Mexico. In February 2001, on his first foreign visit, President Bush came to Mexico to meet with Mexican President Vicente Fox. A requested "deliverable" for that summit meeting was a large partnership training and scholarship program. I was asked to design it. I called the new initiative TIES – Training, Internships, Exchanges, and Scholarships. It supported public–private–nongovernment–university–and community organization partnership programs focused on training. Each project had to have a clear and measurable social and economic development impact that would be furthered through increased sectoral cooperation.

In Mexico, during the Bush Presidency, I developed a significant forest fire mitigation and control program in partnership with the U.S. Forest Service, a large HIV/AIDS control program, maternal and child health cooperation, a sister park environmental partnership for Mexico's protected areas, and U.S.-Mexico biodiversity cooperation with Mexico, Belize, Guatemala, and Honduras on the Mesoamerican Reef and the Mesoamerican Forest, and a Mexico – U..S. initiative to address drug-resistant tuberculosis on the Mexican side of the border.

Walter Mondale, 42nd Vice President of the United States of America and American Ambassador to Japan

My success at the U.S. Embassy in Tokyo resulted from hard work and exquisite support and cooperation from two U.S. Ambassadors - Richard Armacost, who was Ambassador when I was first assigned to the Embassy, and former U.S. Vice President Walter Mondale, who replaced Ambassador Armacost in Tokyo.

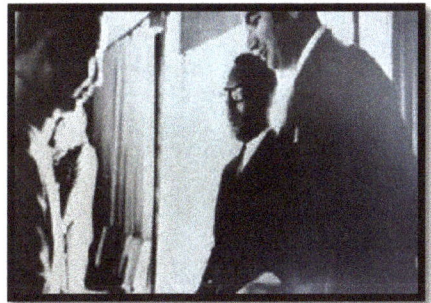

Sisavang Vatthana, King, Kingdom of Laos

The King of Laos knighted me for my work with Hmong and other hill tribe minorities in northern Laos. With its golden three-headed elephant and the white parasol of Buddhism, the certificate was presented to me and my boss at the Royal Palace in Luang Prabang, Laos, on the 14th rising moon day of the 8th lunar month in the Metal Pig year (1971). Earlier in my career, I had met the King during a royal visit to Sam Thong, Xieng Khouang Province where I worked at the teacher training institute. Later, I was transferred from Sam Thong to the royal capital of the Kingdom of Laos, Luang Prabang. The King knighted me at the Royal Palace in Luang Prabang.

General Omar Torrijos, President of the Republic of Panama

After the fall of Indochina to the Communists in 1975, I was transferred by USAID from Southeast Asia to Panama. My background - working with minority hill tribes in Laos and being of Native American descent on my mother's side – made me the "right person at the right time." General Omar Torrijos requested that an American AID officer be assigned to his special unit working on social and economic development for Panama's three main Indian tribes. The Ambassador and USAID Director assigned that project to me.

I worked closely with Panama's Guaymi, Kuna, and Choko tribes in coordination with Colonel Ruben Dario Parades, General Torrijos' Minister of Agriculture. In that capacity, I directed USAID funds and programs toward the three tribes, always considering the goals of the Government of Panama and USAID, and the U.S. Congressional Mandate that required USAID to shift its assistance from the elite to the poorest of the poor.

I traveled with General Torrijos to the Guaymi areas of western Panama and the San Blas island homeland of the Kuna. Watching this charismatic leader in action was a highlight of my service in Latin America.

Henry Kissinger, Secretary of State

Henry Kissinger served as the U.S. Secretary of State from 1973 to 1977 and National Security Advisor from 1960 to 1975. In 1983, President Ronal Reagan appointed Kissinger as the Chair of the National Bipartisan Commission on Central America.

After the Commission Report was issued, my Education and Training Office in USAID/Washington was asked to develop and implement the Commission's recommendations on education and training. This led to a massive expansion of USAID support for education and training in Central America. My office developed various education programs, and I personally developed the Central America Peace Scholarships project and its follow-on expansions.

William Franklin (Billy) Graham, Jr., Ordained Southern Baptist Minister

During my assignment in Tokyo, Japan, as the USAID Representative to the Japanese Official Development Assistance program, I was a part of the Ambassador's Country Team, working closely with the Department of State, EPA, the Department of Commerce, and other U.S. agencies based in the Embassy of the United States in Tokyo.

I was the "right person, at the right place, at the right time." During a visit to Japan, the Reverend Billy Graham was invited to lunch by his close friend, Ambassador Walter Mondale. I was assigned the role of note taker. During the two-hour lunch, I heard the two men discuss topics ranging from civil rights and domestic U.S. politics to foreign affairs. They even talked about religion.

Country preacher Billy Graham, known for his rapid-fire preaching delivery with flailing arms, was nicknamed "The Preaching Windmill." I saw that windmill up close and personal and heard the wit and fire of his faith. It is easy to understand how Billy Graham touched the lives of many millions worldwide with the strength of his character and the power of his message about the love of Jesus.

Mother Theresa, Sisters of Charity, Catholic Saint

In November 1989, the Berlin Wall and the symbolic Iron Curtain fell. Eastern Europe began to open, and in 1991,

U.S. Secretary of State James Baker visited Tirana, Albania. Over 300,000 Albanians welcomed and thanked him. On his return to the U.S., Secretary Baker sent a technical team to analyze development needs and make recommendations to jump-start Albania away from communism and toward democracy. I was on that team. My focus was on education and training.

The challenge was enormous: transforming Albania's education system from its communist orientation to an open-market free orientation at all levels, from preschool through university. All textbooks had to be developed from scratch. I met with Mother Teresa, who was in Albania, to explore possible solutions. Mother Teresa had a solution. Engage the Albanian diaspora in America and elsewhere to translate American textbooks into Albanian. Set up a large, technically expert local committee of Albanian educators to review and approve the translations.

That was done. Albania made a great leap forward toward democracy.

His Holiness, the 14th Dalai Lama, Nobel Laureate, Tenzin Gyatso

The Dalai Lama is the spiritual leader of Tibetan Buddhism. Tibetans believe he is the reincarnation of the Bodhisattva of Compassion. The Dalai Lama dedicates his life to guiding all humans toward enlightenment. He is to Tibetan Buddhism as the Pope is to Roman Catholicism.

I was a duty officer at the U.S. Embassy in Tokyo when the Dalai Lama traveled from India via Tokyo to the United States. At Tokyo's airport, it was discovered that the Dalai Lama's U.S. visa had expired. The Embassy visa section hurriedly issued a valid visa, and my job as a duty officer was to deliver it.

The Dalai Lama's delegation was waiting in a beautiful private room. I met the Dalai Lama's representative. My instructions were clear: only deliver the visa to the Dalai Lama. I was permitted to go into the private area. I met the Dalai Lama and handed him his passport. I had studied Buddhism for many years. I had so much I wanted to say, but I said, "Your Holiness, the new visa."

The Dalai Lama smiled. Seeing my discomfort, he said in his deep voice, "Mind calm. Do Good. Happy! I put my hands together in respect, turned, and euphorically floated from the room.

Paul E. White and Muhammed Ali formed a friendship bond when they met at Al's magic shop in Washington, DC in the 1960s. Both were avid students of magic. Paul and Ali remained friends from that time until Ali's death in 2016. This picture was taken in Tokyo, Japan. Muhammed Ali came to Japan with a large delegation of black leaders, including Coretta Scott King, Andrew Young, Andrew's brother, and many others.

A Muhammed Ali quote summarizes our Brackette family creed or philosophy of life. Brackette ancestors endured much hardship, yet they remained dedicated to a life shaped by respect and love. A Brackette saying is: "There is no room in this world for hate!" Muhammed Ali said it this way: *"Hating people because of their color (or their politics) is wrong. And it doesn't (matter what color (or political group) is doing the hating. It's just plain wrong!"*

The world needs more love and less hate. Brackettes should not fall far from our mighty Brackette oak tree ancestors. Give and receive love. Eschew hatred. This world will be a better place for all!

www.ingramcontent.com/pod-product-compliance
Lightning Source LLC
Chambersburg PA
CBHW051210120626
46547CB00013B/1284